Prayer of the Heart

PRAYER OF THE HEART

Writings from the Philokalia

From the Complete Text compiled by
SAINT NIKODIMOS OF THE HOLY MOUNTAIN
and SAINT MAKARIOS OF CORINTH

Translated from the Greek and edited by
G. E. H. Palmer, Philip Sherrard,
and Kallistos Ware

SHAMBHALA
Boston
1993

Shambhala Publications, Inc.
Horticultural Hall
300 Massachusetts Avenue
Boston, Massachusetts 02115

9 8 7 6 5 4 3 2 1

First Edition

Printed in China on acid-free paper
∞

Distributed in the United States by Random House, Inc.
See page 183 for Library of Congress
Cataloging-in-Publication data.

Contents

Preface

From the Introduction to
The Philokalia: The Complete Text
by G.E.H. Palmer, Philip Sherrard, and Kallistos Ware

The *Philokalia* is a collection of texts written between the fourth and the fifteenth centuries by spiritual masters of the Orthodox Christian tradition. It was compiled in the eighteenth century by two Greek monks, St Nikodimos of the Holy Mountain of Athos (1749–1809) and St Makarios of Corinth (1731–1805), and was first published at Venice in 1782. A second edition was published at Athens in 1893, and this included certain additional texts on prayer by Patriarch Kallistos not found in the 1782 edition. A third edition, in five volumes, was also published at Athens during the years 1957–

1963 by the Astir Publishing Company. It is on the Astir edition that our translation is based.

What first determined the choice of texts made by St Nikodimos and St Makarios, and gives them their cohesion? 'Philokalia' itself means love of the beautiful, the exalted, the excellent, understood as the transcendent source of life and the revelation of Truth. It is through such love that, as the subtitle of the original edition puts it, 'the intellect is purified, illumined and made perfect'. The texts were collected with a view to this purification, illumination and perfection. They show the way to awaken and develop attention and consciousness, to attain that state of watchfulness which is the hallmark of sanctity. They describe the conditions most effective for learning what their authors call the art of arts and the science of sciences, a learning which is not a matter of information or agility of mind but of a radical change of will and heart leading man towards the highest possibilities open to him, shaping and nourishing the unseen part of his being, and helping him to spiritual fulfilment and union with God. The *Philokalia* is an itinerary through the labyrinth of time, a silent way of love and gnosis through the deserts and emptinesses of life, especially of modern life, a vivifying and fadeless presence. It is an active force revealing a spiritual path and inducing man to follow it. It is a summons to him to overcome his ignorance, to uncover the knowledge that lies within, to rid himself of illusion, and to be receptive to the grace of the Holy Spirit who teaches all things and brings all things to remembrance.

Prayer of the Heart

Saint John Cassian

On the Holy Fathers of Sketis
and on Discrimination

Written for Abba Leontios

St John Cassian, often styled 'Cassian the Roman' in Greek sources, was born around the year 360, probably in Roman Scythia. As a young man he joined a monastery in Bethlehem, but around 385–6 he travelled with his friend Germanos to Egypt, where he remained until 399, becoming a disciple of Evagrios. During 401–5 he was at Constantinople, where he was ordained deacon; here he became a disciple and ardent supporter of St John Chrysostom. In 405 he travelled to the West, remaining for some years in Rome and then moving to Gaul. Either in Rome or in Gaul he was ordained priest. Around 415 he founded two monasteries near Marseilles, one for men and the other for women. His two main works are the *Institutes* and the *Conferences*, both written in Latin around the years 425–8. In these Cassian summarized the spiritual teaching which he had received in Egypt, adapting it to the somewhat different conditions of the West. His writings exercised a formative influence on Latin monasticism and are especially commended in the *Rule* of St Benedict. Cassian died around 435 and is commemorated in the Orthodox Church as a saint, his feast-day falling on 29 February.

The promise I made to the blessed Bishop Kastor to give an account of the way of life and the teaching of the holy fathers has been fulfilled in part by the writings I sent him entitled 'On Coenobitic Institutions' and 'On the Eight Vices'; and I now propose to fulfil it completely. But having heard that Bishop Kastor has left us to dwell with Christ, I felt I should send the remaining portion of my treatise to you, most holy Leontios, who have inherited both his virtuous qualities and the guardianship, with God's help, of his monastery.

I and my spiritual friend, the holy Germanos, whom I had known since my youth at school, in the army and in monastic life, were staying in the desert of Sketis, the centre of the most experienced monks. It was there that we saw Abba Moses, a saintly man, outstanding not only in the practice of the virtues but in spiritual contemplation as well. We begged him with tears, therefore, to tell us how we might approach perfection.

After much entreaty on our part, he said: 'Children, all virtues and all pursuits have a certain immediate purpose; and those who look to this purpose and adapt themselves accordingly will reach the ultimate goal to which they aspire. The farmer willingly works the earth, enduring now the sun's heat and now the winter's cold, his immediate purpose being to clear it of thorns and weeds, while his ultimate goal is the enjoyment of its fruits. The merchant, ignoring dangers on land and sea, willingly gives himself to his business with the purpose of making a profit, while his goal is enjoyment of this profit. The soldier, too, ignores the dangers of war and the miseries of service abroad. His purpose is to gain a higher rank by using his ability and skill, while his goal is to enjoy the advantages of this rank.

'Now our profession also has its own immediate purpose and its own ultimate goal, for the sake of which we willingly endure all manner of toil and suffering. Because of this, fasts do not cast us down, the hardship of vigils delights us; the reading and study of Scripture are readily undertaken; and physical work, obedience, stripping oneself of everything earthly, and the life here in this desert are carried out with pleasure.

'You have given up your country, your families, everything worldly in order to embrace a life in a foreign land among rude and uncultured people like us. Tell me, what was your purpose and what goal did you set before yourselves in doing all this?'

We replied: 'We did it for the kingdom of heaven.' In response Abba Moses said: 'As for the goal, you have answered well; but what is the purpose which we set before us and which we pursue unwaveringly so as to reach the kingdom of heaven? This you have not told me.'

When we confessed that we did not know, the old man replied: 'The goal of our profession, as we have said, is the kingdom of God. Its immediate purpose, however, is purity of heart, for without this we cannot reach our goal. We should therefore always have this purpose in mind; and, should it ever happen that for a short time our heart turns aside from the direct path, we must bring it back again at once, guiding our lives with reference to our purpose as if it were a carpenter's rule.

'The Apostle Paul knew this when he said: "Forgetting what lies behind, and reaching forward to what lies in front, I pursue my purpose, aiming at the prize of the high calling of God" (Phil. 3. 13–14). We, too, do everything for the sake of this immediate purpose. We give up country, family, possessions and everything worldly in order to acquire purity of heart. If we forget this purpose we cannot avoid frequently stumbling and losing our way, for we will be walking in the dark and straying from the proper path. This has happened to many men who at the start of their ascetic life gave up all wealth, possessions and everything worldly, but who later flew into a rage over a fork, a needle, a rush or a book. This would not have happened to them had they borne in mind the purpose for which they gave up everything. It is for the love of our neighbour that we scorn wealth, lest by fighting over it and stimulating our disposition to anger, we fall away from love. When we show this disposition to anger towards our brother even in small things, we have lapsed from our purpose and our renunciation of the world is useless. The blessed Apostle was aware of this and said: "Though I give my body to be burned, and have no love, it profits me nothing" (1 Cor. 13: 3). From this we learn that perfection does not follow immediately upon renunciation and withdrawal from the world. It comes after the attainment of love which, as the Apostle said, "is not jealous or puffed up, does not grow angry, bears no grudge, is not arrogant, thinks no evil" (cf. 1

Cor. 13: 4–5). All these things establish purity of heart; and it is for this that we should do everything, scorning possessions, enduring fasts and vigils gladly, engaging in spiritual reading and psalmody. If, however, some necessary task pleasing to God should keep us from our normal fasting and reading, we should not on this account neglect purity of heart. For what we gain by fasting is not so great as the damage done by anger; nor is the profit from reading as great as the harm done when we scorn or grieve a brother.

'Fasts and vigils, the study of Scripture, renouncing possessions and everything worldly are not in themselves perfection, as we have said; they are its tools. For perfection is not to be found in them; it is acquired through them. It is useless, therefore, to boast of our fasting, vigils, poverty, and reading of Scripture when we have not achieved the love of God and our fellow men. Whoever has achieved love has God within himself and his intellect is always with God.'

To this Germanos rejoined: 'What man, while in the flesh, can so fix his intellect on God that he thinks of nothing else, not even of visiting the sick, of entertaining guests, of his handicraft, or of the other unavoidable bodily needs? Above all, since God is invisible and incomprehensible, how can a man's mind always look upon Him and be inseparable from Him?'

Abba Moses replied: 'To look upon God at all times and to be inseparable from Him, in the manner which you envisage, is impossible for a man still in the flesh and enslaved to weakness. In another way, however, it is possible to look upon God, for the manner of contemplating God may be conceived and understood in many ways. God is not only to be known in His blessed and incomprehensible being, for this is something which is reserved for His saints in the age to come. He is also to be known from the grandeur and beauty of His creatures, from His providence which governs the world day by day, from His righteousness and from the wonders which He shows to His saints in each generation. When we reflect on the measurelessness of His power and His unsleeping eye which looks upon the hidden things of the heart and which nothing can escape, we are filled with the deepest awe, marvelling at Him and adoring Him. When we consider that He numbers the raindrops, the sand of the sea and the stars of heaven, we are amazed at the grandeur of His nature and His wisdom. When we think of His ineffable and inexplicable wisdom, His love for mankind, and His limitless long-suffering at man's innumerable sins, we glorify Him. When we consider His great love for us, in that though we had done nothing good He, being God, deigned to become man in order to save us from delusion, we are roused to longing for Him. When we reflect that He Himself has vanquished in us our adversary, the devil, and that He has given us eternal life if only we would choose and turn towards His goodness, then we venerate Him. There are many similar ways of seeing and apprehending God, which grow in us according to our labour and to the degree of our purification.'

Germanos then asked: 'How does it happen

that even against our will many ideas and wicked thoughts trouble us, entering by stealth and undetected to steal our attention? Not only are we unable to prevent them from entering, but it is extremely difficult even to recognize them. Is it possible for the mind to be completely free of them and not be troubled by them at all?'

Abba Moses replied: 'It is impossible for the mind not to be troubled by these thoughts. But if we exert ourselves it is within our power either to accept them and give them our attention, or to expel them. Their coming is not within our power to control, but their expulsion is. The amending of our mind is also within the power of our choice and effort. When we meditate wisely and continually on the law of God, study psalms and canticles, engage in fasting and vigils, and always bear in mind what is to come—the kingdom of heaven, the Gehenna of fire and all God's works—our wicked thoughts diminish and find no place. But when we devote our time to worldly concerns and to matters of the flesh, to pointless and useless conversation, then these base thoughts multiply in us. Just as it is impossible to stop a watermill from turning, although the miller has power to choose between grinding either wheat or tares, so it is impossible to stop our mind, which is ever-moving, from having thoughts, although it is within our power to feed it either with spiritual meditation or with worldly concerns.'

When the old man saw us marvelling at this and still longing to hear more, he was silent for a short while and then said: 'Your longing has made me speak at length, and yet you are still eager for more; and from this I see that you are truly thirsty to be taught about perfection. So I would like to talk to you about the special virtue of discrimination. This is a kind of acropolis or queen among the virtues; and I will show you its excellence and value, not only in my own words, but also through the venerable teachings of the fathers; for the Lord fills His teachers with grace according to the quality and longing of those who listen.

'Discrimination, then, is no small virtue, but one of the most important gifts of the Holy Spirit. Concerning these gifts the Apostle says: "To one is given by the Spirit the principle of wisdom; to another the principle of spiritual knowledge by the same Spirit; to another faith by the same Spirit; to another the gifts of healing . . . to another discrimination of spirits" (1 Cor. 12: 8–10). Then, having completed his catalogue of spiritual gifts, he adds: "But all these are energized by the one and selfsame Spirit" (1 Cor. 12: 11). You can see, therefore, that the gift of discrimination is nothing worldly or insignificant. It is the greatest gift of God's grace. A monk must seek this gift with all his strength and diligence, and acquire the ability to discriminate between the spirits that enter him and to assess them accurately. Otherwise he will not only fall into the foulest pits of wickedness as he wanders about in the dark, but even stumble when his path is smooth and straight.

'I remember how in my youth, when I was in the Thebaid, where the blessed Antony used to live, some elders came to see him, to enquire with him into the question of perfection in virtue. They asked him: "Which is the greatest of all virtues—we mean the virtue capable of keeping a monk from being harmed by the nets of the devil and his deceit?" Each one then gave his opinion according to his understanding. Some said that fasting and the keeping of vigils make it easier to come near to God, because these refine and purify the mind. Others said that voluntary poverty and detachment from personal possessions make it easier, since through these the mind is released from the intricate threads of worldly care. Others judged acts of compassion to be the most important, since in the Gospel the Lord says: "Come, you whom my Father has blessed, inherit the kingdom prepared for you from the foundation of the world; for I was hungry and you gave Me food" and so on (Matt. 25: 34–36). The best part of the night was passed in this manner, taken up with a discussion in which each expressed his opinion as to which virtue makes it easiest for a man to come near to God.

'Last of all the blessed Antony gave his reply: "All that you have said is both necessary and helpful for those who are searching for God and wish to come to Him. But we cannot award the first place to any of these virtues; for there are many among us who have endured fasting and vigils, or have withdrawn into the desert, or have practised poverty to such an extent that they have not left themselves enough for their daily sustenance, or have performed acts of compassion so generously that they no longer have anything to give; and yet these same monks, having done all this, have nevertheless fallen away miserably from virtue and slipped into vice.

' "What was it, then, that made them stray from the straight path? In my opinion it was simply that they did not possess the grace of discrimination; for it is this virtue that teaches a man to walk along the royal road, swerving neither to the right through immoderate self-control, nor to the left through indifference and laxity. Discrimination is a kind of eye and lantern of the soul, as is said in the gospel passage: 'The light of the body is the eye; if therefore your eye is pure, your whole body will be full of light. But if your eye is evil, your whole body will be full of darkness' (Matt. 6: 22–3). And this is just what we find; for the power of discrimination, scrutinizing all the thoughts and actions of a man, distinguishes and sets aside everything that is base and not pleasing to God, and keeps him free from delusion.

' "We can see this in what is said in the Holy Scriptures. Saul, the first to be entrusted with the kingship of Israel, did not have the eye of discrimination; so his mind was darkened and he was unable to perceive that it was more pleasing to God that he should obey the commandment of Samuel than that he should offer sacrifices. He gave offence through the very things with which he thought to serve God, and because of them he was deposed. This would not have happened had he possessed the light of discrimination (cf. 1 Sam. 13: 8–9).

' "The Apostle calls this virtue 'the sun', as we can see from his saying: 'Do not let the sun go down upon your anger' (Eph. 4: 26). It is also called 'the guidance' of our lives, as when it is written: 'those who have no guidance fall like leaves' (Prov. 11: 14. LXX). Scripture also refers to it as the 'discernment' without which we must do nothing—not even drink the spiritual wine that 'makes glad the heart of man' (Ps. 104: 15. LXX); for it is said: 'Drink with discernment' (Prov. 31: 3. LXX); and: 'He that does not do all things with discernment is like a city that is broken down and without walls' (Prov. 25: 28. LXX). Wisdom, intellection and perceptiveness are united in discrimination: and without these our inner house cannot be built, nor can we gather spiritual wealth; for it is written: 'Through wisdom a house is built, through understanding it is established, and through good judgment its storehouses will be filled with wealth' (Prov. 24: 3–4. LXX). Discrimination is also called the 'solid food' that 'is suitable for those who have their organs of perception trained by practice to discriminate between good and evil' (Heb. 5: 14). These passages show very clearly that without the gift of discrimination no virtue can stand or remain firm to the end, for it is the mother of all the virtues and their guardian." '

Saint Theodoros the Great Ascetic

Theoretikon

A Century of Spiritual Texts and *Theoretikon* are ascribed in the Greek *Philokalia* to St Theodoros the Great Ascetic, a monk of the monastery of St Sabas near Jerusalem, who subsequently became bishop of Edessa in Syria (commemorated in the church calendar on 19 July). Historically he remains a shadowy figure, since his *Life,* written by Basil of Emesa, is often untrustworthy. Whereas St Nikodimos dates him to the seventh century, probably he should be placed two centuries later.

The *Century* may be the work of St Theodoros, but the *Theoretikon* almost certainly is not. Largely a free paraphrase of Evagrios, the *Century* is not earlier than the seventh century, since it draws on St Maximos the Confessor's teaching concerning self-love, and not later than the beginning of the eleventh century, since it is found in a manuscript of 1023; a ninth-century date is therefore possible. The *Theoretikon*, a valuable summary of the spiritual life, is hard to fix chronologically, but it is undoubtedly much later than the *Century*. Its style and outlook suggest perhaps a fourteenth-century date, but it may even be as recent as the seventeenth century, which would make it one of the latest texts in the *Philokalia*. It is apparently incomplete, lacking both opening and conclusion.

What an immense struggle it is to break the fetter binding us so strongly to material things, to stop worshipping these things, and to acquire instead a state of holiness. Indeed, unless our soul is truly noble and courageous it cannot embark on such a task. For our goal is not merely the purification of the passions: this by itself is not real virtue, but preparation for virtue. To purification from vicious habits must be added the acquisition of the virtues.

With respect to its intelligent aspect, to purify the soul is to eradicate and completely expunge from it all degrading and distorted features, all 'worldly cares', as the Divine Liturgy puts it, all turbulence, evil tendencies and senseless prepossessions. With respect to its desiring aspect, it is to purge away every impulsion towards what is material, to cease from viewing things according to the senses, and to be obedient to the intelligence. And with respect to the soul's incensive power, purification consists in never being perturbed by anything that happens.

In the wake of this purification, and the mortification or correction of ugly features, there should follow spiritual ascent and deification. For after abandoning what is evil, one must practise what is good. One must first deny oneself and then, taking up the cross, must follow the Master towards the supreme state of deification.

What are ascent and deification? For the intellect, they are perfect knowledge of created things, and of Him who is above created things, so far as such knowledge is accessible to human nature. For the will, they are total and continuous striving towards primal goodness. And for the incensive power, they are energetic and effective impulsion towards the object of aspiration, persistent, relentless, and unarrested by any practical difficulties, pressing forward impetuously and undeviatingly.

The soul's impulsion towards beauty should surpass its impulsion towards what is base to the same degree as intelligible beauty surpasses sensible beauty. One should provide the body only with what is needed to keep it functioning properly. To intend to do this is easy, but to achieve it is more difficult, for without great effort one cannot uproot the soul's well-entrenched habits.

Nor indeed is knowledge to be acquired without effort. Certainly, to keep one's vision intently fixed on divine things until the will acquires the habit of doing this requires considerable labour over a long period of time. The intellect has to exert itself to oppose the downward drag of the senses; and this contest and battle against the body continues until death, even if it seems to diminish as anger and desire wither away, and as the senses are subjugated to the transcendent knowledge of the intellect.

It should be remarked, however, that an unillumined soul, since it has no help from God, can neither be genuinely purified, nor ascend to the divine light. What was said above refers to those who are baptized.

Moreover, a distinction should be made between different kinds of knowledge. Knowledge here on earth is of two kinds: natural and supranatural. The second can be understood by reference to the first. Natural knowledge is that which the soul can acquire through the use of its natural faculties and powers when investigating creation and the cause of creation—in so far, of course, as this is possible for a soul bound to matter. For, when speaking of the senses, the imagination and the intellect, it has to be said that the energy of the intellect is blunted by being joined and mingled with the body. As a result, it cannot have direct contact with intelligible forms, but requires, in order to apprehend them, the imagination, which by nature uses images, and shares in material extension and density. Accordingly, the intellect while in the flesh needs to use material images in order to apprehend intelligible forms. We call natural knowledge, then, whatever knowledge the intellect in such a state acquires by its own natural means.

Supranatural knowledge, on the other hand, is that which enters the intellect in a manner transcending its own means and power; that is to say, the intelligible objects that constitute such knowledge surpass the capacity of an intellect joined to a body, so that a knowledge of them pertains naturally only to an intellect which is free from the body. Such knowledge is infused by God alone when He finds an intellect purified of all material attachment and inspired by divine love.

Not only knowledge but virtue as well is divided in this way. One kind of virtue does not transcend nature, and this can fittingly be called natural virtue. The other, which is energized only by the primal source of beauty, is above our natural capacity and state; and this kind of virtue should be called supranatural.

Knowledge and virtue, then, are divided in this way. An unillumined person may possess natural knowledge and virtue, but never those which are supranatural. How could he, since he does not participate in their energizing cause? But the illumined man can possess both. Moreover, although he cannot acquire supranatural virtue at all unless he has first acquired natural virtue, he can participate in supranatural knowledge without first acquiring natural knowledge. In addition, just as sense and imagination are far superior and more noble in man than they are in animals, so natural virtue and knowledge are far superior and more noble in the person who is illumined than in the person who is unillumined, although both may possess them.

Further, that aspect of natural knowledge concerned with the virtues and with the habits opposing them also seems to be of two kinds. One kind is theoretical knowledge, when a man speculates about these matters but lacks experience of them, and is sometimes unsure about what he says. The other is practical and, so to speak, alive, since the knowledge in question is confirmed by experience, and so is clear and trustworthy, and in no way uncertain or doubtful.

In view of all this, there appear to be four obstacles which hinder the intellect in the acquisition of virtue. First, there is prepossession, that is, the ingrained influence of habits running counter to virtue; and this, operative over a long period, exerts a pressure which drags the intellect down towards earthly things. Secondly, there is the action of the senses, stimulated by sensible beauty and drawing the intellect after it. Thirdly, there is the dulling of noetic energy due to the intellect's connection with the body. The intellect of an embodied soul is not related to an intelligible object in the same way as sight is to a visible object or, in general, the senses are to sensory objects. Immaterial intellects apprehend intelligible objects more effectively than sight apprehends visible objects. But just as faulty sight visualizes its images of natural objects somewhat indistinctly and unclearly, so does our intellect, when embodied, apprehend intelligible objects. And since it cannot now clearly discern intelligible beauties, it cannot aspire after them either. For one has a longing for something only to the degree that one possesses knowledge of it. Hence the intellect—since it cannot help being drawn towards what appears to be beautiful, whether or not it really is so—is drawn down to sensible beauty, for this now makes a clearer impression on it.

The fourth of the obstacles impeding the intellect in its acquisition of virtue is the pernicious influence of unclean and hostile demons. It is impossible to speak of all the various snares they set on the spiritual path, making use of the senses, the reason, the intellect—in fact, of everything that exists. If He who carries the lost sheep on His shoulders (cf. Luke 15: 5) did not in His infinite care protect those who turn to Him, not a single soul would escape.

Three things are needed in order to overcome these obstacles. The first and most important thing is to look to God with our whole soul, to ask for help from His hand, and to put all our trust in Him, knowing full well that without His assistance we shall inevitably be dragged away from Him. The second—which I regard as an overture to the first—is constantly to nourish the intellect with knowledge. By knowledge I mean that of all created things, sensible and intelligible, both as they are in themselves and with reference to the primal Source, since they derive from it and are related to it; and in addition to this, the contemplation, as far as is possible, of the Cause of all created things, through the qualities that appertain to Him. To be concerned with the nature of created things has a very purifying effect. It frees us from passionate attachment to them and from delusion about them; and it is the surest of means for raising our soul to the Source of all. For all beauty, miracle, magnificence reflects what is supremely beautiful, miraculous and magnificent—reflects, rather, the Source that is above beauty, miracle and magnificence.

If the mind is always occupied with these things, how can it not long for supernal goodness itself? If it can be drawn to what is alien to it, how will it not be far more strongly drawn to what is cognate? When the soul cleaves to what is kindred to it, how can it turn away from what it loves to anything inferior? It will even resent its incarnate life, finding it a hindrance to the attaining of the beautiful. For though the intellect, while living in matter, beholds intelligible beauty but dimly, yet intelligible blessings are such that even a slight emanation from that overflowing beauty, or a faint vision of it, can impel the intellect to soar beyond all that is outside the intelligible realm, and to aspire to that alone, never letting itself lapse from the delight it offers, come what distress there may.

The third way by which we can overcome the obstacles already mentioned is to mortify our partner, the body; for otherwise we cannot attain a clear and distinct vision of the intelligible world. The flesh is mortified or, rather, crucified with Christ, through fasting, vigils, sleeping on the ground, wearing coarse clothing and only what is essential, through suffering and toil. In this fashion it is refined and purified, made light and subtle, readily and unresistingly following the guidance of the intellect and rising upwards with it. Without such mortification all our efforts are vain.

When these three holy ways are established in mutual harmony, they beget in the soul the choir of blessed virtues; for those whom they adorn are free from all trace of sin and blessed with every virtue. Yet the rejection of material wealth, or of fame, may distress the intelligence; for the soul, still bound to such things, is pierced by many passions. None the less I firmly maintain that a soul attached to wealth and praise cannot mount upwards. Equally I say that a soul loses all attachment to these things once it has practised this triad of ways sufficiently for it to have become habitual. For if the soul is persuaded that only the beauty which is beyond everything is to be regarded as truly beautiful, while of other things the most beautiful is that which is most like the supreme beauty, and so on down the scale, how can it relish silver, gold or fame, or any other degrading thing?

Even what most holds us back—I mean our cares and concerns—is no exception to the rule. For what cares will a man have, if he is not attached to anything worldly or involved with it? The cloud of cares comes from the fumes, so to speak, of the main passions—self-indulgence, avarice, love of praise. Once you are free of these you will also have cast off your cares.

Sound moral judgment has the same effect as wisdom, and is a most powerful factor drawing us upwards. Hence it too has its part to play. For the knowledge of the virtues involves the most scrupulous discrimination between good and evil; and this requires sound moral judgment. Experience and the struggle with the body teach us how to use such judgment in our warfare.

Fear also comes into the argument. For the greater our longing for God the greater grows our fear; and the more we hope to attain God, the more we fear Him. If we are wounded by divine love, the sting of fear exceeds that of a thousand threats of punishment. For as nothing is more blessed than to attain God, so nothing is more terrible than this great fear of losing Him.

To come to another point: everything may be understood in terms of its purpose. It is this that determines the division of everything into its constituent parts, as well as the mutual relationship of those parts. Now the purpose of our life is blessedness or, what is the same thing, the kingdom of heaven or of God. This is not only to behold the Trinity, supreme in Kingship, but also to receive an influx of the divine and, as it were, to suffer deification; for by this influx what is lacking and imperfect in us is supplied and perfected. And the provision by such divine influx of what is needed is the food of spiritual beings. There is a kind of eternal circle, which ends where it begins. For the greater our noetic perception, the more we long to perceive; and the greater our longing, the greater our enjoyment; and the greater our enjoyment, the more our perception is deepened, and so the motionless movement, or the motionless immobility, begins again. Such then is our purpose, in so far as we can understand it. We must now see how we can attain it.

To intelligent souls, which as intellective

beings are only a little lower than angelic intellects, life in this world is a struggle and incarnate life an open contest. The prize of victory is the state we have described, a gift worthy both of God's goodness and of His justice: of His justice, because these blessings are attained not without our own sweat; of His goodness, because His boundless generosity surpasses all our toil—especially as the very capacity for doing good and the actual doing of it are themselves gifts of God.

What, then, is the nature of our contest in this world? The intelligent soul is conjoined with an animal-like body, which has its being from the earth and gravitates downwards. It is so mixed with the body that though they are total opposites they form a single being. Without change or confusion in either of them, and with each acting in accordance with its nature, they compose a single person, or hypostasis, with two complete natures. In this composite two-natured being, man, each of his natures functions in accordance with its own particular powers. It is characteristic of the body to desire what is akin to it. This longing for what is akin to them is natural to created beings, since indeed their existence depends on the intercourse of like with like, and on their enjoyment of material things through the senses. Then, being heavy, the body welcomes relaxation. These things are proper and desirable for our animal-like nature. But to the intelligent soul, as an intellective entity, what is natural and desirable is the realm of intelligible realities and its enjoyment of them in the manner characteristic of it. Before and above all what is characteristic of the intellect is an intense longing for God. It desires to enjoy Him and other intelligible realities, though it cannot do this without encountering obstacles.

The first man could indeed, without any hindrance, apprehend and enjoy sensory things by means of the senses and intelligible things with the intellect. But he should have given his attention to the higher rather than to the lower, for he was as able to commune with intelligible things through the intellect, as he was with sensory things through the senses. I do not say that Adam ought not to have used the senses, for it was not for nothing that he was invested with a body. But he should not have indulged in sensory things. When perceiving the beauty of creatures, he should have referred it to its source and as a consequence have found his enjoyment and his wonder fulfilled in that, thus giving himself a twofold reason for marvelling at the Creator. He should not have attached himself, as he did, to sensory things and have lost himself in wonder at them, neglecting the Creator of intelligible beauty.

Thus Adam used the senses wrongly and was spellbound by sensory beauty; and because the fruit appeared to him to be beautiful and good to eat (Gen. 3: 6), he tasted it and forsook the enjoyment of intelligible things. So it was that the just Judge judged him unworthy of what he had rejected—the contemplation of God and of created beings—and, making darkness His secret place (cf. 2 Sam. 22: 12; Ps. 18: 11), deprived him of Himself and of immaterial realities. For holy things must not be made available to the impure. What he fell in love with, God permitted him to enjoy, allowing him to live according to the senses, with but faint vestiges of intellectual perception.

Henceforward our struggle against the things of this world became harder, because it is now no longer in our power to enjoy intelligible realities in a way corresponding to that in which we enjoy sensory realities with the senses, even though we are greatly assisted by baptism, which purifies and exalts us. Yet, in so far as we can, we must give our attention to the intelligible and not to the sensible world. We must reverence it and aspire to it; but we must not reverence any sensory object in and for itself, or try to enjoy it in that way; for in truth what is sensory cannot compare with what is intelligible. Just as the essence of the one far excels that of the other, so does its beauty. To aspire to what is ugly rather than to what is beautiful, to what is ignoble rather than to what is noble, is sheer lunacy. And if that is the case where both sensible and intelligible creations are involved, how much more so is it when we prefer matter, formless and ugly, to God Himself.

This, then, is our contest and struggle: strictly to watch ourselves, so that we always strive to enjoy intelligible realities, directing intellect and appetite to that end, and never allowing them secretly to be beguiled by the senses into revering sensory things for their own sake. And if we have to use the senses, we should use them in order to grasp the Creator through His creation, seeing Him reflected in created things as the sun is reflected in water, since in their inner beings they are in varying degrees images of the primal cause of all.

Such, then, is our aim. How can we achieve it? As we said, the body desires to enjoy through the senses what is akin to it; and the stronger it is, the stronger its desire. But this conflicts with the soul's purpose. So the soul must make every effort to curb the senses, so that we do not indulge in sensible realities in the way described. But since the stronger the body, the stronger its desire, and the stronger its desire the harder it is to check, the soul must mortify the body through fasting, vigils, standing, sleeping on the ground, going unwashed, and through every other kind of hardship, thus reducing its strength and making it tractable and obedient to the soul's noetic activities. This is the aim. Yet it is easy to wish, hard to achieve; and failures greatly outnumber the successes, because even if we are most attentive, the senses often beguile us. So a third remedy has been devised: prayer and tears. Prayer gives thanks for blessings received and asks for failures to be forgiven and for power to strengthen us for the future; for without God's help the soul can indeed do nothing. None the less, to persuade the will to have the strongest possible desire for union with and enjoyment of Him, for whom it longs, and to direct itself totally towards Him, is the major part of the achievement of our aim. And tears too have great power. They gain God's mercy for our faults, purify us of the defilements produced through sensual pleasures, and spur our desire upwards.

Thus, our aim is the contemplation of intelligible realities and total aspiration towards them. The mortification of the flesh, together with the fasting, self-restraint and other things that contribute to it, are all practised as a means to this end. And in their company is prayer. Each has many aspects; some contribute to one thing, some to another.

Love of praise and love of material wealth must not be regarded as pertaining to the body. Only the love of sensual pleasure pertains to the body. The fitting remedy for this is bodily hardship. Love of praise and love of material wealth are the progeny of ignorance. Having no experience of true blessings and no knowledge of noetic realities, the soul has adopted such bastard offspring, thinking that riches can supply its needs. Also it plunges after material wealth in order to satisfy its love for pleasure and praise, and even for its own sake, as if such wealth were a blessing in itself. All this results from ignorance of true blessings. Love of praise does not derive from any lack on the part of the body, for it satisfies no physical need. Inexperience and ignorance of primal goodness and true glory give rise to it. Indeed, ignorance is the root of all evils. For no one who has once grasped as he should the true nature of things—from where each thing comes and how it is perverted—can then totally disregard his own purpose and be dragged down to worldly things. The soul does not want a good that is only apparent. And if it is under the sway of some habit, it is also quite able to overcome this habit. Yet even before the habit was formed it had been deceived by ignorance. Hence one should above all strive after a true knowledge of created beings, and then spur one's will towards primal goodness, scorning all worldly things and aware of their great vanity. For what do they contribute to our own true purpose?

To sum up briefly. An intelligent soul, while in the body, has but one task: to realize its own purpose. But since the will's energy remains unstimulated unless there is intellection, we begin by trying to energize noetically. Noetic activity is either for the sake of willing or, more commonly, for its own sake as well as for the sake of willing. Blessedness—of which any significant life on earth is not only an overture but also a prefiguration—is characterized by both energies: by both intellection and willing, that is, by both love and spiritual pleasure. Whether both these energies are supreme, or one is superior to the other, is open to discussion. For the moment we shall regard both of them as supreme. One we call contemplative and the other practical. Where these supreme energies are concerned, the one cannot be found without the other. In the case of the lower energies, sequent to these two, each may be found singly. Whatever hinders these two energies, or opposes them, we call vice. Whatever fosters them, or frees them from obstacles, we call virtue. Energies that spring from the virtues are good; those that spring from their opposites are distorted and sinful. The supreme goal, whose energy, as we know, is compound of intellection and willing, endows each particular energy with a specific form, which may be used for either good or evil.

Saint Maximos the Confessor

First Century on Love

The extreme importance of St Maximos the Confessor (580–662) for the Orthodox spiritual tradition is indicated by the fact that no other writer is assigned so much space in the *Philokalia*. A member of the aristocracy, after receiving an elaborate education St Maximos served at first in the civil service, perhaps as secretary to the Emperor Heraklios. Around 614 he became a monk at the monastery of Philippikos in Chrysopolis (Scutari), close to Constantinople, subsequently moving to another monastery not far distant at Cyzikos (Erdek). In 626, at the time of the Persian invasion, he fled to Crete and eventually to Africa, where he remained for some years. From 633–4 onwards he played a leading part in opposing the heresies of Monoenergism and Monotheletism, and because of this he was arrested in 653 by the imperial authorities, brought to Constantinople for trial, and sent into exile. Further trials and condemnations followed, the last being at Constantinople in 662, after which he was flogged, his tongue was plucked out and his right hand cut off. He died soon afterwards as an exile in the Caucasus. His memorial is observed in the Orthodox Church on 21 January, and also on the day of his death, 13 August.

I. Love is a holy state of the soul, disposing it to value knowledge of God above all created things. We cannot attain lasting possession of such love while we are still attached to anything worldly.

2. Dispassion engenders love, hope in God engenders dispassion, and patience and forbearance engender hope in God; these in turn are the product of complete self-control, which itself springs from fear of God. Fear of God is the result of faith in God.

3. If you have faith in the Lord you will fear punishment, and this fear will lead you to control the passions. Once you control the passions you will accept affliction patiently, and through such acceptance you will acquire hope in God. Hope in God separates the intellect from every worldly attachment, and when the

intellect is detached in this way it will acquire love for God.

4. The person who loves God values knowledge of God more than anything created by God, and pursues such knowledge ardently and ceaselessly.

5. If everything that exists was made by God and for God, and God is superior to the things made by Him, he who abandons what is superior and devotes himself to what is inferior shows that he values things made by God more than God Himself.

6. When your intellect is concentrated on the love of God you will pay little attention to visible things and will regard even your own body as something alien.

7. Since the soul is more noble than the body and God incomparably more noble than

the world created by Him, he who values the body more than the soul and the world created by God more than the Creator Himself is simply a worshipper of idols.

8. If you distract your intellect from its love for God and concentrate it, not on God, but on some sensible object, you thereby show that you value the body more than the soul and the things made by God more than God Himself.

9. Since the light of spiritual knowledge is the intellect's life, and since this light is engendered by love for God, it is rightly said that nothing is greater than divine love (cf. 1 Cor. 13).

10. When in the intensity of its love for God the intellect goes out of itself, then it has no sense of itself or of any created thing. For when it is illumined by the infinite light of God, it becomes insensible to everything made by Him,

just as the eye becomes insensible to the stars when the sun rises.

11. All the virtues co-operate with the intellect to produce this intense longing for God, pure prayer above all. For by soaring towards God through this prayer the intellect rises above the realm of created beings.

12. When the intellect is ravished through love by divine knowledge and stands outside the realm of created beings, it becomes aware of God's infinity. It is then, according to Isaiah, that a sense of amazement makes it conscious of its own lowliness and in all sincerity it repeats the prophet's words: 'How abject I am, for I am pierced to the heart; because I am a man of unclean lips, and I dwell among a people of unclean lips; and my eyes have seen the King, the Lord of hosts' (Isa. 6: 5).

13. The person who loves God cannot help loving every man as himself, even though he is grieved by the passions of those who are not yet purified. But when they amend their lives, his delight is indescribable and knows no bounds.

14. A soul filled with thoughts of sensual desire and hatred is unpurified.

15. If we detect any trace of hatred in our hearts against any man whatsoever for committing any fault, we are utterly estranged from love for God, since love for God absolutely precludes us from hating any man.

16. He who loves Me, says the Lord, will keep My commandments (cf. John 14: 15, 23); and 'this is My commandment, that you love one another' (John 15: 12). Thus he who does not love his neighbour fails to keep the commandment, and so cannot love the Lord.

17. Blessed is he who can love all men equally.

18. Blessed is he who is not attached to anything transitory or corruptible.

19. Blessed is the intellect that transcends all sensible objects and ceaselessly delights in divine beauty.

20. If you make provision for the desires of the flesh (cf. Rom. 13: 14) and bear a grudge against your neighbour on account of something transitory, you worship the creature instead of the Creator.

21. If you keep your body free from disease and sensual pleasure it will help you to serve what is more noble.

22. He who forsakes all worldly desires sets himself above all worldly distress.

23. He who loves God will certainly love his

neighbour as well. Such a person cannot hoard money, but distributes it in a way befitting God, being generous to everyone in need.

24. He who gives alms in imitation of God does not discriminate between the wicked and the virtuous, the just and the unjust, when providing for men's bodily needs. He gives equally to all according to their need, even though he prefers the virtuous man to the bad man because of the probity of his intention.

25. God, who is by nature good and dispassionate, loves all men equally as His handiwork. But He glorifies the virtuous man because in his will he is united to God. At the same time, in His goodness He is merciful to the sinner and by chastising him in this life brings him back to the path of virtue. Similarly, a man of good and dispassionate judgment also loves all men

equally. He loves the virtuous man because of his nature and the probity of his intention; and he loves the sinner, too, because of his nature and because in his compassion he pities him for foolishly stumbling in darkness.

26. The state of love may be recognized in the giving of money, and still more in the giving of spiritual counsel and in looking after people in their physical needs.

27. He who has genuinely renounced worldly things, and lovingly and sincerely serves his neighbour, is soon set free from every passion and made a partaker of God's love and knowledge.

28. He who has realized love for God in his heart is tireless, as Jeremiah says (cf. Jer. 17: 16. LXX), in his pursuit of the Lord his God, and bears every hardship, reproach and insult nobly,

never thinking the least evil of anyone.

29. When you are insulted by someone or humiliated, guard against angry thoughts, lest they arouse a feeling of irritation, and so cut you off from love and place you in the realm of hatred.

30. You should know that you have been greatly benefited when you have suffered deeply because of some insult or indignity; for by means of the indignity self-esteem has been driven out of you.

31. Just as the thought of fire does not warm the body, so faith without love does not actualize the light of spiritual knowledge in the soul.

32. Just as the light of the sun attracts a healthy eye, so through love knowledge of God naturally draws to itself the pure intellect.

33. A pure intellect is one divorced from

ignorance and illumined by divine light.

34. A pure soul is one freed from passions and constantly delighted by divine love.

35. A culpable passion is an impulse of the soul that is contrary to nature.

36. Dispassion is a peaceful condition of the soul in which the soul is not easily moved to evil.

37. A man who has been assiduous in acquiring the fruits of love will not cease loving even if he suffers a thousand calamities. Let Stephen, the disciple of Christ, and others like him persuade you of the truth of this (cf. Acts 7: 60). Our Lord Himself prayed for His murderers and asked the Father to forgive them because they did not know what they were doing (cf. Luke 23: 34).

38. If love is long-suffering and kind (cf. 1

Cor. 13: 4), a man who is contentious and malicious clearly alienates himself from love. And he who is alienated from love is alienated from God, for God is love.

39. Do not say that you are the temple of the Lord, writes Jeremiah (cf. Jer. 7: 4); nor should you say that faith alone in our Lord Jesus Christ can save you, for this is impossible unless you also acquire love for Him through your works. As for faith by itself, 'the devils also believe, and tremble' (Jas. 2: 19).

40. We actively manifest love in forbearance and patience towards our neighbour, in genuinely desiring his good, and in the right use of material things.

41. He who loves God neither distresses nor is distressed with anyone on account of transitory things. There is only one kind of distress

which he both suffers and inflicts on others: that salutary distress which the blessed Paul suffered and which he inflicted on the Corinthians (cf. 2 Cor. 7: 8–11).

42. He who loves God lives the angelic life on earth, fasting and keeping vigils, praying and singing psalms and always thinking good of every man.

43. If a man desires something, he makes every effort to attain it. But of all things which are good and desirable the divine is incomparably the best and the most desirable. How assiduous, then, we should be in order to attain what is of its very nature good and desirable.

44. Stop defiling your flesh with shameful deeds and polluting your soul with wicked thoughts; then the peace of God will descend upon you and bring you love.

45. Afflict your flesh with hunger and vigils and apply yourself tirelessly to psalmody and prayer; then the sanctifying gift of self-restraint will descend upon you and bring you love.

46. He who has been granted divine knowledge and has through love acquired its illumination will never be swept hither and thither by the demon of self-esteem. But he who has not yet been granted such knowledge will readily succumb to this demon. However, if in all that he does he keeps his gaze fixed on God, doing everything for His sake, he will with God's help soon escape.

47. He who has not yet attained divine knowledge energized by love is proud of his spiritual progress. But he who has been granted such knowledge repeats with deep conviction the words uttered by the patriarch Abraham

when he was granted the manifestation of God: 'I am dust and ashes' (Gen. 18: 27).

48. The person who fears the Lord has humility as his constant companion and, through the thoughts which humility inspires, reaches a state of divine love and thankfulness. For he recalls his former worldly way of life, the various sins he has committed and the temptations which have befallen him since his youth; and he recalls, too, how the Lord delivered him from all this, and how He led him away from a passion-dominated life to a life ruled by God. Then, together with fear, he also receives love, and in deep humility continually gives thanks to the Benefactor and Helmsman of our lives.

49. Do not befoul your intellect by clinging to thoughts filled with anger and sensual desire. Otherwise you will lose your capacity for pure

prayer and fall victim to the demon of list-lessness.

50. When the intellect associates with evil and sordid thoughts it loses its intimate communion with God.

51. The foolish man under attack from the passions, when stirred to anger, is senselessly impelled to leave his brethren. But when heated by desire he quickly changes his mind and seeks their company. An intelligent person behaves differently in both cases. When anger flares up he cuts off the source of disturbance and so frees himself from his feeling of irritation against his brethren. When desire is uppermost he checks every unruly impulse and chance conversation.

52. In time of trial do not leave your monastery but stand up courageously against the

thoughts that surge over you, especially those of irritation and listlessness. For when you have been tested by afflictions in this way, according to divine providence, your hope in God will become firm and secure. But if you leave, you will show yourself to be worthless, unmanly and fickle.

53. If you wish not to fall away from the love of God, do not let your brother go to bed feeling irritated with you, and do not go to bed yourself feeling irritated with him. Reconcile yourself with your brother, and then come to Christ with a clear conscience and offer Him your gift of love in earnest prayer (cf. Matt. 5: 24).

54. St Paul says that, if we have all the gifts of the Spirit but do not have love, we are no further forward (cf. 1 Cor. 13: 2). How assidu-

ous, then, we ought to be in our efforts to acquire this love.

55. If 'love prevents us from harming our neighbour' (Rom. 13: 10), he who is jealous of his brother or irritated by his reputation, and damages his good name with cheap jibes or in any way spitefully plots against him, is surely alienating himself from love and is guilty in the face of eternal judgment.

56. If 'love is the fulfilling of the law' (Rom. 13: 10), he who is full of rancour towards his neighbour and lays traps for him and curses him, exulting in his fall, must surely be a transgressor deserving eternal punishment.

57. If 'he who speaks evil of his brother, and judges his brother, speaks evil of the law, and judges the law' (Jas. 4: 11), and the law of Christ is love, surely he who speaks evil of Christ's

love falls away from it and is the cause of his own perdition.

58. Do not listen gleefully to gossip at your neighbour's expense or chatter to a person who likes finding fault. Otherwise you will fall away from divine love and find yourself cut off from eternal life.

59. Do not permit any abuse of your spiritual father or encourage anyone who dishonours him. Otherwise the Lord will be angry with your conduct and will obliterate you from the land of the living (cf. Deut. 6: 15).

60. Silence the man who utters slander in your hearing. Otherwise you sin twice over: first, you accustom yourself to this deadly passion and second, you fail to prevent him from gossiping against his neighbour.

61. 'But I say to you,' says the Lord, 'love

your enemies . . . do good to those who hate you, and pray for those who mistreat you' (Matt. 5: 44). Why did He command this? To free you from hatred, irritation, anger and rancour, and to make you worthy of the supreme gift of perfect love. And you cannot attain such love if you do not imitate God and love all men equally. For God loves all men equally and wishes them 'to be saved and to come to the knowledge of the truth' (1 Tim. 2: 4).

62. 'But I say to you, do not resist evil; but if someone hits you on the right cheek, turn to him the other cheek as well. And if anyone sues you in the courts, and takes away your coat, let him have your cloak also. And if anyone forces you to go a mile, go with him for two miles' (Matt. 5: 39–41). Why did He say this? Both to keep you free from anger and irritation, and to

correct the other person by means of your forbearance, so that like a good Father He might bring the two of you under the yoke of love.

63. We carry about with us impassioned images of the things we have experienced. If we can overcome these images we shall be indifferent to the things which they represent. For fighting against the thoughts of things is much harder than fighting against the things themselves, just as to sin in the mind is easier than to sin through outward action.

64. Some passions pertain to the body, others to the soul. The first are occasioned by the body, the second by external objects. Love and self-control overcome both kinds, the first curbing the passions of the soul and the second those of the body.

65. Some passions pertain to the soul's in-

censive power, and others to its desiring aspect. Both kinds are aroused through the senses. They are aroused when the soul lacks love and self-control.

66. The passions of the soul's incensive power are more difficult to combat than those of its desiring aspect. Consequently our Lord has given a stronger remedy against them: the commandment of love.

67. While passions such as forgetfulness and ignorance affect but one of the soul's three aspects—the incensive, the desiring or the intelligent—listlessness alone seizes control of all the soul's powers and rouses almost all the passions together. That is why this passion is more serious than all the others. Hence our Lord has given us an excellent remedy against it, saying: 'You will gain possession of your

souls through your patient endurance' (Luke 21: 19).

68. Never strike any of the brethren, especially without reason, in case he is unable to bear the affliction and leaves the monastery. For then you would never escape the reproach of your conscience. It would always bring you distress in the time of prayer and divert your intellect from intimate communion with God.

69. Shun all suspicions and all persons that cause you to take offence. If you are offended by anything, whether intended or unintended, you do not know the way of peace, which through love brings the lovers of divine knowledge to the knowledge of God.

70. You have not yet acquired perfect love if your regard for people is still swayed by their characters—for example, if, for some particular

reason, you love one person and hate another, or if for the same reason you sometimes love and sometimes hate the same person.

71. Perfect love does not split up the single human nature, common to all, according to the diverse characteristics of individuals; but, fixing attention always on this single nature, it loves all men equally. It loves the good as friends and the bad as enemies, helping them, exercising forbearance, patiently accepting whatever they do, not taking the evil into account at all but even suffering on their behalf if the opportunity offers, so that, if possible, they too become friends. If it cannot achieve this, it does not change its own attitude; it continues to show the fruits of love to all men alike. It was on account of this that our Lord and God Jesus Christ, showing His love for us, suffered for the

whole of mankind and gave to all men an equal hope of resurrection, although each man determines his own fitness for glory or punishment.

72. If you are not indifferent to both fame and dishonour, riches and poverty, pleasure and distress, you have not yet acquired perfect love. For perfect love is indifferent not only to these but even to this fleeting life and to death.

73. Listen to the words of those who have been granted perfect love: 'What can separate us from the love of Christ? Can affliction, or distress, or persecution, or famine, or nakedness, or peril, or the sword? As it is written, "For Thy sake we are put to death all the day long; we are regarded as sheep for slaughtering" (Ps. 44: 22). But in all these things we are more than conquerors through Him that loved us. For I am convinced that neither death, nor life,

nor angels, nor principalities, nor powers, nor things present, nor things to come, nor height, nor depth, nor any other created thing, can separate us from the love of God that is in Christ Jesus our Lord' (Rom. 8: 35–39). Those who speak and act thus with regard to divine love are all saints.

74. Listen now to what they say about love for our neighbour: 'I speak the truth in Christ, I do not lie, my conscience also bears me witness in the Holy Spirit: I have great distress and continual sorrow in my heart. For I could wish that I myself were severed from Christ for the sake of my brethren, my kinsmen according to the flesh, who are Israelites' (Rom. 9: 1–3). Moses and the other saints speak in a similar manner.

75. He who is not indifferent to fame and

pleasure, as well as to the love of riches that exists because of them and increases them, cannot cut off occasions for anger. And he who does not cut these off cannot attain perfect love.

76. Humility and ascetic hardship free a man from all sin, for the one cuts out the passions of the soul, the other those of the body. This is what the blessed David indicates when he prays to God, saying, 'Look on my humility and my toil, and forgive all my sins' (Ps. 25: 18).

77. It is through our fulfilling of the commandments that the Lord makes us dispassionate; and it is through His divine teachings that He gives us the light of spiritual knowledge.

78. All such teachings are concerned either with God, or with things visible and invisible,

or else with the providence and judgment relating to them.

79. Almsgiving heals the soul's incensive power; fasting withers sensual desire; prayer purifies the intellect and prepares it for the contemplation of created beings. For the Lord has given us commandments which correspond to the powers of the soul.

80. 'Learn from Me', He said, 'for I am gentle and humble in heart' (Matt. 11: 29). Gentleness keeps the soul's incensive power in a calm state; humility frees the intellect from conceit and self-esteem.

81. Fear of God is of two kinds. The first is generated in us by the threat of punishment. It is through such fear that we develop in due order self-control, patience, hope in God and dispassion; and it is from dispassion that love

comes. The second kind of fear is linked with love and constantly produces reverence in the soul, so that it does not grow indifferent to God because of the intimate communion of its love.

82. The first kind of fear is expelled by perfect love when the soul has acquired this and is no longer afraid of punishment (cf. 1 John 4: 18). The second kind, as we have already said, is always found united with perfect love. The first kind of fear is referred to in the following two verses: 'Out of fear of the Lord men shun evil' (Prov. 16: 6), and 'Fear of the Lord is the beginning of wisdom' (Ps. 111: 10). The second kind is mentioned in the following verses: 'Fear of the Lord is pure, and endures for ever' (Ps. 19: 9. LXX), and 'Those who fear the Lord will not want for anything' (Ps. 34: 10. LXX).

83. 'Put to death therefore whatever is earthly in you: unchastity, uncleanness, passion, evil desire and greed' (Col. 3: 5). Earth is the name St Paul gives to the will of the flesh. Unchastity is his word for the actual committing of sin. Uncleanness is how he designates assent to sin. Passion is his term for impassioned thoughts. By evil desire he means the simple act of accepting the thought and the desire. And greed is his name for what generates and promotes passion. All these St Paul ordered us to mortify as 'aspects' expressing the will of the flesh.

84. First the memory brings some passion-free thought into the intellect. By its lingering there, passion is aroused. When the passion is not eradicated, it persuades the intellect to assent to it. Once this assent is given, the actual

sin is then committed. Therefore, when writing to converts from paganism, St Paul in his wisdom orders them first to eliminate the actual sin and then systematically to work back to the cause. The cause, as we have already said, is greed, which generates and promotes passion. I think that greed in this case means gluttony, because this is the mother and nurse of unchastity. For greed is a sin not only with regard to possessions but also with regard to food, just as self-control likewise relates to both food and possessions.

85. When a sparrow tied by the leg tries to fly, it is held back by the string and pulled down to the earth. Similarly, when the intellect that has not yet attained dispassion flies up towards heavenly knowledge, it is held back by the passions and pulled down to the earth.

86. The intellect, once totally free from passions, proceeds undistracted to the contemplation of created beings, making its way towards knowledge of the Holy Trinity.

87. When in a pure state, the intellect, on receiving the conceptual images of things, is moved to contemplate these things spiritually. But when it is sullied through indolence, while its conceptual images may in general be free from passion, those concerned with people produce in it thoughts that are shameful or wicked.

88. When during prayer no conceptual image of anything worldly disturbs your intellect, then know that you are within the realm of dispassion.

89. Once the soul starts to feel its own good

health, the images in its dreams are also calm and free from passion.

90. Just as the physical eye is attracted to the beauty of things visible, so the purified intellect is attracted to the knowledge of things invisible. By things invisible, I mean things incorporeal.

91. It is already much not to be roused to any passion by material things. It is even more to remain dispassionate when presented with mental images of such things. For the war which the demons wage against us by means of thoughts is more severe than the war they wage by means of material things.

92. He who has succeeded in attaining the virtues and is enriched with spiritual knowledge sees things clearly in their true nature. Conse-

quently, he both acts and speaks with regard to all things in a manner which is fitting, and he is never deluded. For according to whether we use things rightly or wrongly we become either good or bad.

93. If the conceptual images that continually rise up in the heart are free from passion whether the body is awake or asleep, then we may know that we have attained the highest state of dispassion.

94. Through fulfilling the commandments the intellect strips itself of the passions. Through spiritual contemplation of things visible it casts off impassioned conceptions of such things. Through knowledge of things invisible it discards the contemplation of things visible. Finally it denudes itself even of this through knowledge of the Holy Trinity.

95. When the sun rises and casts its light on the world, it reveals both itself and the things it illumines. Similarly, when the Sun of righteousness rises in the pure intellect, He reveals both Himself and the inner principles of all that has been and will be brought into existence by Him.

96. We do not know God from His essence. We know Him rather from the grandeur of His creation and from His providential care for all creatures. For through these, as though they were mirrors, we may attain insight into His infinite goodness, wisdom and power.

97. The pure intellect is occupied either with passion-free conceptual images of human affairs, or with the natural contemplation of things visible or invisible, or with the light of the Holy Trinity.

98. When the intellect is engaged in the contemplation of things visible, it searches out either the natural principles of these things or the spiritual principles which they reflect, or else it seeks their original cause.

99. When the intellect is absorbed in the contemplation of things invisible, it seeks their natural principles, the cause of their generation and whatever follows from this, as well as the providential order and judgment which relates to them.

100. When the intellect is established in God, it at first ardently longs to discover the principles of His essence. But God's inmost nature does not admit of such investigation, which is indeed beyond the capacity of everything created. The qualities that appertain to His nature, however, are accessible to the intel-

lect's longing: I mean the qualities of eternity, infinity, indeterminateness, goodness, wisdom, and the power of creating, preserving and judging creatures. Yet of these, only infinity may be grasped fully; and the very fact of knowing nothing is knowledge surpassing the intellect, as the theologians Gregory of Nazianzos and Dionysios have said.

A DISCOURSE ON ABBA PHILIMON

The *Discourse* that follows, unlike most of the material in the *Philokalia*, is narrative in form; doubtless it was included by the editors because of the long and important passages on inward meditation and on watchfulness. Apart from what is recorded in the present text, nothing is known about Abba Philimon. The *Discourse*, while stating that he lived in Egypt and was a priest, provides no clear indication of his date. Certainly he was earlier than the twelfth century, since the *Discourse* is mentioned by St Peter of Damaskos. Egypt seems in Philimon's day to be still part of the Roman Empire, which suggests that he lived in the sixth century, or at the latest in the early seventh just before the Arab conquest. The Jesus Prayer is cited by Philimon in what has come to be regarded as its standard form, 'Lord Jesus Christ, Son of God, have mercy upon me': the *Discourse* seems to be the earliest source to cite explicitly this precise formula.

I t is said that Abba Philimon, the anchorite, lived for a long time enclosed in a certain cave not far from the Lavra of the Romans. There he engaged in the life of ascetic struggle, always asking himself the question which, it is reported, the great Arsenios used to put to himself: 'Philimon, why did you come here?' He used to plait ropes and make baskets, giving them to the steward of the Lavra in exchange for a small ration of bread. He ate only bread and salt, and even that not every day. In this way he took no thought for the flesh (cf. Rom. 13: 14) but, initiated into ineffable mysteries through the pursuit of contemplation, he was enveloped by divine light and established in a state of joyfulness. When he went to church on Saturdays and Sundays he walked alone in deep thought, allowing no one to approach him lest his concentration should be interrupted. In church he stood in a corner, keeping his face turned to the ground and shedding streams of tears. For, like the holy fathers, and especially like his great model Arsenios, he was always full of contrition and kept the thought of death continually in his mind.

When a heresy arose in Alexandria and the surrounding area, Philimon left his cave and went to the Lavra near that of Nikanor. There he was welcomed by the blessed Paulinos, who gave him his own retreat and enabled him to follow a life of complete stillness. For a whole year Paulinos allowed absolutely no one to approach him, and he himself disturbed him only when he had to give him bread.

On the feast of the holy resurrection of Christ, Philimon and Paulinos were talking when the subject of the eremitical state came up. Philimon knew that Paulinos, too, aspired to this state; and with this in mind he implanted in him teachings taken from Scripture and the fathers that emphasized, as Moses had done, how impossible it is to conform to God without complete stillness; how stillness gives birth to ascetic effort, ascetic effort to tears, tears to awe, awe to humility, humility to foresight, foresight to love; and how love restores the soul to health and makes it dispassionate, so that one then knows that one is not far from God.

He used to say to Paulinos: 'You must purify your intellect completely through stillness and engage it ceaselessly in spiritual work. For just as the eye is attentive to sensible things and is fascinated by what it sees, so the purified intellect is attentive to intelligible realities and becomes so rapt by spiritual contemplation that it is hard to tear it away. And the more the intellect is stripped of the passions and purified through stillness, the greater the spiritual knowledge it is found worthy to receive. The intellect is perfect when it transcends knowledge of created things and is united with God: having then attained a royal dignity it no longer allows itself to be pauperized or aroused by lower desires, even if offered all the kingdoms of the world. If, therefore, you want to acquire all these virtues, be detached from every man, flee the world and sedulously follow the path of the saints. Dress shabbily, behave simply, speak unaffectedly, do not be haughty in the way you walk, live in poverty and let yourself be despised by everyone. Above all, guard the intellect and be watchful, patiently enduring indigence and hardship, and keeping intact and undisturbed the spiritual blessings that you have been granted. Pay strict attention to yourself, not allowing any sensual pleasure to infiltrate. For the soul's passions are allayed by stillness; but when they are stimulated and aroused they grow more savage and force us into greater sin; and they become hard to cure, like the body's wounds when they are scratched and chafed. Even an idle word can make the intellect forget God, the demons enforcing this with the compliance of the senses.

'Great struggle and awe are needed to guard the soul. You have to divorce yourself from the whole world and sunder your soul's affection for the body. You have to become citiless, homeless, possessionless, free from avarice, from worldly concerns and society, humble, compassionate, good, gentle, still, ready to receive in your heart the stamp of divine knowledge. You cannot write on wax unless you have first expunged the letters written on it. Basil the Great teaches us these things.

'The saints were people of this kind. They were totally severed from the ways of the world, and by keeping the vision of heaven unsullied in themselves they made its light shine by observing the divine laws. And having mortified their earthly aspects (cf. Col. 3: 5) through self-control and through awe and love for God, they were radiant with holy words and actions. For through unceasing prayer and the study of the divine Scriptures the soul's noetic eyes are opened, and they see the King of the celestial powers, and great joy and fierce longing burn intensely in the soul; and as the flesh, too, is taken up by the Spirit, man becomes wholly spiritual. These are the things which those who in solitude practise blessed stillness and the strictest way of life, and who have separated themselves from all human solace, confess openly to the Lord in heaven alone.'

When the good brother heard this, his soul was wounded by divine longing; and he and

Abba Philimon went to live in Sketis where the greatest of the holy fathers had pursued the path of sanctity. They settled in the Lavra of St John the Small, and asked the steward of the Lavra to see to their needs, as they wished to lead a life of stillness. And by the grace of God they lived in complete stillness, unfailingly attending church on Saturdays and Sundays but on other days of the week staying in their cells, praying and fulfilling their rule.

The rule of the holy Elder was as follows. During the night he quietly chanted the entire Psalter and the Biblical canticles, and recited part of the Gospels. Then he sat down and intently repeated 'Lord have mercy' for as long as he could. After that he slept, rising towards dawn to chant the First Hour. Then he again sat down, facing eastward, and alternately chanted psalms and recited by heart sections of the Epistles and Gospels. He spent the whole day in this manner, chanting and praying unceasingly, and being nourished by the contemplation of heavenly things. His intellect was often lifted up to contemplation, and he did not know if he was still on earth.

His brother, seeing him devoted so unremittingly to this rule and completely transformed by divine thoughts, said to him: 'Why, father, do you exhaust yourself so much at your age, disciplining your body and bringing it into subjection?' (cf. 1 Cor. 9: 27). And he replied: 'Believe me, my son, God has placed such love for my rule in my soul that I lack the strength to satisfy the longing within me. Yet longing for God and hope of the blessings held in store triumph over bodily weakness.' Thus at all times, even when he was eating, he raised his intellect up to the heavens on the wings of his longing.

Once a certain brother who lived with him asked him: 'What is the mystery of contemplation?' Realizing that he was intent on learning, the Elder replied: 'I tell you, my son, that when one's intellect is completely pure, God reveals to him the visions that are granted to the ministering powers and angelic hosts.' The same brother also asked: 'Why, father, do you find more joy in the psalms than in any other part of divine Scripture? And why, when quietly chanting them, do you say the words as though you were speaking with someone?' And Abba Philimon replied: 'My son, God has impressed the power of the psalms on my poor soul as He did on the soul of the prophet David. I cannot be separated from the sweetness of the visions about which they speak: they embrace all Scripture.' He confessed these things with great humility, after being much pressed, and then only for the benefit of the questioner.

A brother named John came from the coast to Father Philimon and, clasping his feet, said to him: 'What shall I do to be saved? For my intellect vacillates to and fro and strays after all the wrong things.' After a pause, the father replied: 'This is one of the outer passions and it stays with you because you still have not acquired a perfect longing for God. The warmth of this longing and of the knowledge of God has not yet come to you.' The brother said to him: 'What shall I do, father?' Abba Philimon replied: 'Meditate inwardly for a while, deep in your heart; for this can cleanse your intellect of these things.' The brother, not understanding what was said, asked the Elder: 'What is inward meditation, father?' The Elder replied: 'Keep watch in your heart; and with watchfulness say in your mind with awe and trembling: "Lord Jesus Christ, have mercy upon me." For this is the advice which the blessed Diadochos gave to beginners.'

The brother departed; and with the help of God and the Elder's prayers he found stillness and for a while was filled with sweetness by this meditation. But then it suddenly left him and he could not practise it or pray watchfully. So he went again to the Elder and told him what had happened. And the Elder said to him: 'You have had a brief taste of stillness and inner work, and have experienced the sweetness that comes from them. This is what you should always be doing in your heart: whether eating or drinking, in company or outside your cell, or on a journey, repeat that prayer with a watchful mind and an undeflected intellect; also chant, and meditate on prayers and psalms. Even when carrying out needful tasks, do not let your intellect be idle but keep it meditating inwardly and praying. For in this way you can grasp the depths of divine Scripture and the power hidden in it, and give unceasing work to the intellect, thus fulfilling the apostolic command: "Pray without ceasing" (1 Thess. 5: 17). Pay strict attention to your heart and watch over it, so that it does not give admittance to thoughts that are evil or in any way vain and useless. Without interruption, whether asleep or awake, eating, drinking, or in company, let your heart inwardly and mentally at times be meditating on the psalms, at other times be repeating the prayer, "Lord Jesus Christ, Son of God, have mercy upon me." And when you chant, make sure that your mouth is not saying one thing while your mind is thinking about another.'

Again the brother said: 'In my sleep I see many vain fantasies.' And the Elder said to him: 'Don't be sluggish or neglectful. Before going to sleep, say many prayers in your heart, fight against evil thoughts and don't be deluded by the devil's demands; then God will receive you into His presence. If you possibly can, sleep only after reciting the psalms and after inward meditation. Don't be caught off your guard, letting your mind admit strange thoughts; but lie down meditating on the thought of your prayer, so that when you sleep it may be conjoined with you and when you awake it may commune with you (cf. Prov. 6: 22). Also, recite the holy Creed of the Orthodox faith before you fall asleep. For true belief in God is the source and guard of all blessings.'

On another occasion the brother asked Abba Philimon: 'In your love, father, explain to me the work in which your intellect is engaged. Then I too may be saved.' And the Elder said: 'Why are you curious about these things?' The brother got up and, clasping and kissing the saint's feet, he begged for an answer. After a long time, the Elder said: 'You cannot yet grasp it: for only a person established in righteousness can give to each of the senses the work proper to it. And you have to be completely purged of vain worldly thoughts before you are found worthy of this gift. So if you want such things, practise the inward meditation with a pure heart. For if you pray ceaselessly and meditate on the Scriptures, your soul's noetic eyes are opened, and there is great joy in the soul and a certain keen and ineffable longing, even the flesh being kindled by the Spirit, so that the whole man becomes spiritual. Whether it is at night or during the day that God grants you the gift of praying with a pure intellect, undistractedly, put aside your own rule, and reach towards God with all your strength, cleaving to Him. And He will illumine your heart about the spiritual work which you should undertake.' And he added: 'A certain elder once came to me and, on my asking him about the state of his intellect, he said: "For two years I entreated God in my whole heart, unremittingly asking Him to imprint in my heart continuously and undistractedly the prayer which He Himself gave to His disciples; and seeing my struggle and patient endurance, the munificent Lord granted me this request." '

Abba Philimon also said this: 'Thoughts about vain things are sicknesses of an idle and sluggish soul. We must, then, as Scripture enjoins, guard our intellect diligently (cf. Prov. 4: 23), chanting undistractedly and with understanding, and praying with a pure intellect. God wants us to show our zeal for Him first by our outward asceticism, and then by our love and unceasing prayer; and He provides the path of salvation. The only path leading to heaven is that of complete stillness, the avoidance of all evil, the acquisition of blessings, perfect love towards God and communion with Him in holiness and righteousness. If a man has attained these things he will soon ascend to the divine realm. Yet the person who aspires to this realm must first mortify his earthly aspects (cf. Col. 3: 5). For when our soul rejoices in the contemplation of true goodness, it does not return to any of the passions energized by sensual or bodily pleasure; on the contrary, it turns away from all such pleasure and receives the manifestation of God with a pure and undefiled mind.

'It is only after we have guarded ourselves rigorously, endured bodily suffering and purified the soul, that God comes to dwell in our hearts, making it possible for us to fulfil His commandments without going astray. He Himself will then teach us how to hold fast to His laws, sending forth His own energies, like rays of the sun, through the grace of the Spirit implanted in us. By way of trials and sufferings we must purify the divine image in us in accordance with which we possess intelligence and are able to receive understanding and the likeness to God; for it is by reforging our senses in the furnace of our trials that we free them from all defilement and assume our royal dignity. God created human nature a partaker of every divine blessing, able to contemplate spiritually the angelic choirs, the splendour of the dominions, the spiritual powers, principalities and authorities, the unapproachable light, and the refulgent glory. Should you achieve some virtue, do not regard yourself as superior to your brother, thinking that you have succeeded whereas he has been negligent; for this is the beginning of pride. Be extremely careful not to do anything simply in order to gain the esteem or goodwill of others. When you are struggling with some passion, do not flinch or become apathetic if the battle continues; but rise up and cast yourself before God, repeating with all your heart the prophet's words, "O Lord, judge those who injure me (Ps. 35: 1. LXX); for I cannot defeat them." And He, seeing your humility, will quickly send you His help. And when you are walking along the road with someone, do not indulge in idle talk, but keep your intellect employed in the spiritual work in which it was previously engaged, so that this work becomes habitual to it and makes it forget worldly pleasures, anchoring it in the harbour of dispassion.'

When he had taught the brother these and many other things, Abba Philimon let him go. But after a short time the brother came back to him and began questioning him, saying: 'What must I do, father? During my night rule sleep weighs me down and does not allow me to pray with inner watchfulness, or to keep vigil beyond the regular period. And when I sing psalms, I want to take up manual work.' Abba Philimon said: 'When you are able to pray with inner watchfulness, do not engage in manual work. But if you are weighed down by listlessness, move about a little, so as to rid yourself of it, and take up manual work.'

The brother again asked him: 'Father, are you not yourself weighed down by sleep while practising your rule?' He replied: 'Hardly ever. But if sleep does sometimes lay hold on me a little, I move about and recite from the Gospel of John, from the beginning, turning the mind's eyes towards God; and sleepiness at once disappears. I do the same with regard to evil thoughts: when such a thought comes, I encounter it like fire with tears, and it disappears. You cannot as yet defend yourself in this manner; but always meditate inwardly and say the daily prayers laid down by the holy fathers. By this I mean, try to recite the Third, Sixth, and Ninth Hours, Vespers and the night services. And, so far as you can, do nothing simply to gain the esteem or goodwill of others, and never bear ill will towards your brother, lest you separate yourself from God. Strive to keep your mind undistracted, always being attentive to your inner thoughts. When you are in church, and are going to partake of the divine mysteries of Christ, do not go out until you have attained complete peace. Stand in one place, and do not leave it until the dismissal.

Think that you are standing in heaven, and that in the company of the holy angels you are meeting God and receiving Him in your heart. Prepare yourself with great awe and trembling, lest you mingle with the holy powers unworthily.' Arming the brother with these counsels and commending him to the Lord and to the Spirit of His grace (cf. Acts 20: 32), Abba Philimon let him go.

The brother who lived with the Abba also related the following: 'Once, as I sat near him, I asked him whether he had been tempted by the wiles of the demons while dwelling in the desert. And he replied: "Forgive me, brother; but if God should let the temptations to which I have been subjected by the devil come to you, I do not think you would be able to bear their venom. I am in my seventieth year, or older.

Enduring a great number of trials while dwelling in extreme stillness in solitary places, I was much tempted and suffered greatly. But nothing is to be gained by speaking of such bitter things to people who as yet have no experience of stillness. When tempted, I always did this: I put all my hope in God, for it was to Him that I made my vows of renunciation. And He at once delivered me from all my distress. Because of this, brother, I no longer take thought for myself. I know that He takes thought for me, and so I bear more lightly the trials that come upon me. The only thing I offer from myself is unceasing prayer. I know that the more the suffering, the greater the reward for him who endures it. It is a means to reconciliation with the righteous Judge.

' "Aware of this, brother, do not grow slack.

Recognize that you are fighting in the thick of the battle and that many others, too, are fighting for us against God's enemy. How could we dare to fight against so fearful an enemy of ·mankind unless the strong right arm of the Divine Logos upheld us, protecting and sheltering us? How could human nature withstand his ploys? 'Who', says Job, 'can strip off his outer garment? And who can penetrate the fold of his breastplate? Burning torches pour from his mouth, he hurls forth blazing coals. Out of his nostrils come smoke of burning soot, with the fire of charcoal. His breath is charcoal, a flame comes from his mouth, power lodges in his neck. Destruction runs before him. His heart is hard as stone, it stands like an unyielding anvil. He makes the deep boil like a cauldron; he regards the sea as a pot of ointment, and the nether deep as a captive. He sees every high thing; and he is king of all that is in the waters' (Job 41: 13, 19–22, 24, 31–32, 34. LXX). This passage describes the monstrous tyrant against whom we fight. Yet those who lawfully engage in the solitary life soon defeat him: they do not possess anything that is his; they have renounced the world and are resolute in virtue; and they have God fighting for them. Who has turned to the Lord with awe and has not been transformed in his nature? Who has illumined himself with the light of divine laws and actions, and has not made his soul radiant with divine intellections and thoughts? His soul is not idle, for God prompts his intellect to long insatiably for light. Strongly energized in this way, the soul is not allowed by the spirit to grow flabby with the passions; but like a king who, full of fire and fury against his enemies, strikes them mercilessly and never retreats, it emerges triumphant, lifting its hands to heaven through the practice of the virtues and the prayer of the intellect." '

The same brother also spoke as follows about the Elder: 'In addition to his other virtues, Abba Philimon possessed this characteristic: he would never listen to idle talk. If someone inadvertently said something which was of no benefit to the soul, he did not respond at all. When I went away on some duty, he did not ask: "Why are you going away?"; nor, when I returned, did he ask: "Where are you coming from?" Or "What have you been doing?" Once, indeed, I had to go to Alexandria by ship; and from there I went to Constantinople on a church matter. I said goodbye to the brethren at Alexandria, but told Abba Philimon nothing about my journey. After spending quite a time in Constantinople, I returned to him in Sketis. When he saw me, he was filled with joy and, after greeting me, he said a prayer. Then he sat down and, without asking me anything at all, continued his contemplation.

'On one occasion, wanting to test him, for days I did not give him any bread to eat. And he did not ask for any, or say anything. After this I bowed low to him and said: "Tell me, father, were you distressed that I did not bring you your food, as I usually do?" And he replied: "Forgive me, brother, even if for twenty days you did not bring me any bread, I would not ask you for it: so long as my soul can last out, so can my body." To such a degree was he absorbed in the contemplation of true goodness.'

'He also used to say: "Since I came to Sketis, I have not allowed my thought to go beyond my cell; nor have I permitted my mind to dwell on anything except the fear of God and the judgment of the age to be; for I have meditated only on the sentence which threatens sinners, on the eternal fire and the outer darkness, on the state of the souls of sinners and of the righteous, and on the blessings laid up for the righteous, each receiving 'his own payment for his own labour' (1 Cor. 3: 8): one for his growing load of suffering, another for his acts of compassion and for his unfeigned love, another for his total shedding of possessions and renunciation of the whole world, another for his humility and consummate stillness, another for his extreme obedience, another for his voluntary exile. Pondering these things, I constrain all other thoughts; and I can no longer be with people or concern my intellect with them, lest I be cut off from more divine meditations."

'He also spoke of a certain solitary who had attained dispassion and used to receive bread from the hand of an angel; but he grew negligent and so was deprived of this honour. For when the soul slackens the intellect's concentration, darkness comes over it. Where God does not illumine, everything is confused, as in darkness; and the soul is unable to look only at God and tremble at His words. "I am a God close at hand, says the Lord, not a distant God. Can a man hide himself in secret, and I not see him? Do I not fill heaven and earth? says the Lord"

(Jer. 23: 23–24. LXX). He also recalled many others who had similar experiences, among them Solomon. For Solomon, he said, had received such wisdom and been so glorified by men that he was like the morning-star and illumined all with the splendour of his wisdom; yet for the sake of a little sensual pleasure he lost that glory (cf. 1 Kings 11: 1–11). Negligence is to be dreaded. We must pray unceasingly lest some thought comes and separates us from God, distracting our intellect from Him. For the pure heart, being completely receptive to the Holy Spirit, mirrors God in His entirety.

'When I heard these things', said the brother, 'and saw his actions, I realized that all fleshly passions were inoperative in him. His desire was always fixed on higher things, so that he was continually transformed by the divine

Spirit, sighing with "cries that cannot be uttered" (Rom. 8: 26), concentrating himself within himself, assessing himself, and struggling to prevent anything from clouding his mind's purity and from defiling him imperceptibly.

'Seeing all this and spurred to emulate his achievements, I was continually prompted to question him. "How, like you, can I acquire a pure intellect?" I asked. And he replied: "You have to struggle. The heart has to strive and to suffer. Things worth striving and suffering for do not come to us if we sleep or are indolent. Even earth's blessings do not come to us without effort on our part. If you want to develop spiritually you must above all renounce your own will; you must acquire a heart that is sorrowful and must rid yourself of all possessions, giving attention not to the sins of others but to your own sins, weeping over them day and night; and you must not be emotionally attached to anyone. For a soul harrowed by what it has done and pricked to the heart by the memory of past sins, is dead to the world and the world to it; that is to say, all passions of the flesh become inoperative, and man becomes inoperative in relation to them. For he who renounces the world, ranging himself with Christ and devoting himself to stillness, loves God; he guards the divine image in himself and enriches his likeness to God, receiving from Him the help of the Spirit and becoming an abode of God and not of demons; and he acts righteously in God's sight. A soul purified from the world and free from the defilements of the flesh, 'having no spot or wrinkle' (Eph. 5: 27), will win the crown of righteousness and shine with the beauty of virtue.

' "But if when you set out on the path of renunciation there is no sorrow in your heart, no spiritual tears or remembrance of endless punishment, no true stillness or persistent prayer, no psalmody and meditation on the divine Scriptures; if none of these things has become habitual in you, so that whether you like it or not they are forced on you by the unremitting perseverance of the intellect; and if awe of God does not grow in your mind, then you are still attached to the world and your intellect cannot be pure when you pray. True devoutness and awe of God purify the soul from the passions, render the intellect free, lead it to natural contemplation, and make it apt for theology. This it experiences in the form of bliss, that provides those who share in it with a foretaste of the bliss held in store and keeps the soul in a state of tranquillity.

' "Let us, then, do all we can to cultivate the virtues, for in this way we may attain true devoutness, that mental purity whose fruit is natural and theological contemplation. As a great theologian puts it, it is by practising the virtues that we ascend to contemplation. Hence, if we neglect such practice we will be destitute of all wisdom. For even if we reach the height of virtue, ascetic effort is still needed in order to curb the disorderly impulses of the body and to keep a watch on our thoughts. Only thus may Christ to some small extent dwell in us. As we develop in righteousness, so we develop in spiritual courage; and when the intellect has been perfected, it unites wholly with God and is illumined by divine light, and the most hidden mysteries are revealed to it. Then it truly learns where wisdom and power lie, and that understanding which comprehends everything, and 'length of days and life, and the light of the eyes and peace' (Baruch 3: 14). While it is still fighting against the passions it cannot as yet enjoy these things. For virtues and vices blind the intellect: vices prevent it from seeing the virtues, and virtues prevent it from seeing vices. But once the battle is over and it is found worthy of spiritual gifts, then it becomes wholly luminous, powerfully energized by grace and rooted in the contemplation of spiritual realities. A person in whom this happens is not attached to the things of this world but has passed from death to life.

' "The person pursuing the spiritual life and

drawing close to God must, therefore, have a chaste heart and a pure tongue so that his words, in their purity, are fit for praising God. A soul that cleaves to God continuously communes with Him.

' "Thus, brethren, let our desire be to attain the summit of the virtues, and not to remain earth-bound and attached to the passions. For the person engaged in spiritual struggle who has drawn close to God, who partakes of the holy light and is wounded by his longing for it, delights in the Lord with an inconceivable spiritual joy. It is as the psalm says: 'Delight in the Lord, and may He grant you the petitions of your heart . . . May He reveal your righteousness like the light, and your judgment like the noonday' (cf. Ps. 37: 4, 6. LXX). For what longing of the soul is as unbearably strong as that which God promotes in it when it is purged of every vice and sincerely declares: 'I am wounded by love' (Song of Songs 5: 8. LXX)? The radiance of divine beauty is wholly inexpressible: words cannot describe it, nor the ear grasp it. To compare the true light to the rays of the morning star or the brightness of the moon or the light of the sun is to fail totally to do justice to its glory and is as inadequate as comparing a pitch-black moonless night to the clearest of noons. This is what St Basil, the great teacher, learnt from experience and subsequently taught us." '

The brother who lived with Abba Philimon related these and many other things. But equally wonderful, and a great proof of his humility, is the fact that, although Abba Philimon had long been a presbyter and both his conduct and knowledge were of a celestial order, he held back from fulfilling his priestly functions to such an extent that in his many years of spiritual struggles he hardly ever consented to approach the altar; and in spite of the strictness of his life, he never partook of the divine mysteries if he had been talking with other people, even though he had not said anything worldly and he had spoken only to help those who questioned him. When he was going to partake of the divine mysteries, he supplicated God with prayers, chanting, and confession of sins. During the service, he was full of fear when the priest intoned the words, 'Holy things to the holy.' For he used to say that the whole church was then filled with holy angels, and that the King of the celestial powers Himself was invisibly celebrating, transformed in our hearts into body and blood. It was on account of this that he said that we should dare to partake of the immaculate mysteries of Christ only when in a chaste and pure state, as it were outside the flesh and free from all hesitation and doubt; in this way we would participate in the illumination that comes from them. Many of the holy fathers saw angels watching over them, and so they maintained silence, not entering into conversation with anyone.

The brother also said that when Abba Philimon had to sell his handiwork, he pretended to be a fool, in case speaking and answering questions might lead him into some lie, or oath, or chatter, or some other kind of sin. Whenever anyone bought anything he simply paid what he thought fit. The Abba, this truly wise man, made small baskets, and accepted gratefully whatever was given, saying absolutely nothing.

THEOPHANIS THE MONK

The Ladder of Divine Graces

*Which Experience Has Made Known to Those
Inspired by God*

In the Greek *Philokalia* this poem appears without any introductory note, and nothing is known concerning its author. He lays particular emphasis upon the need for direct personal experience. Eternal life, he also insists, has to begin here and now, in this present world; but at the same time, like St Gregory of Nyssa, he sees perfection as an endless progress in the age to come, 'a step that has no limit'.

The first step is that of purest prayer.
From this there comes a warmth of heart,
And then a strange, a holy energy,
Then tears wrung from the heart, God-given.
Then peace from thoughts of every kind.
From this arises purging of the intellect,
And next the vision of heavenly mysteries.
Unheard-of light is born from this ineffably,
And thence, beyond all telling, the heart's illu-
   mination.
Last comes—a step that has no limit
Though compassed in a single line—
Perfection that is endless.
The ladder's lowest step
Prescribes pure prayer alone.
But prayer has many forms:
My discourse would be long
Were I now to speak of them:

And, friend, know that always
Experience teaches one, not words.
A ladder rising wondrously to heaven's vault:
Ten steps that strangely vivify the soul.
Ten steps that herald the soul's life.
A saint inspired by God has said:
Do not deceive yourself with idle hopes
That in the world to come you will find life
If you have not tried to find it in this present
    world.
Ten steps: a wisdom born of God.
Ten steps: fruit of all the books.
Ten steps that point towards perfection.
Ten steps that lead one up to heaven.
Ten steps through which a man knows God.
The ladder may seem short indeed,
But if your heart can inwardly experience it
You will find a wealth the world cannot contain,

A god-like fountain flowing with unheard-of
    life.
This ten-graced ladder is the best of masters,
Clearly teaching each to know its stages.
If when you behold it
You think you stand securely on it,
Ask yourself on which step you stand,
So that we, the indolent, may also profit.
My friend, if you want to learn about all this,
Detach yourself from everything,
From what is senseless, from what seems intel-
    ligent.
Without detachment nothing can be learnt.
Experience alone can teach these things, not
    talk.
Even if these words once said
By one of God's elect strike harshly,
I repeat them to remind you:

He who has no foothold on this ladder,
Who does not ponder always on these things,
When he comes to die will know
Terrible fear, terrible dread,
Will be full of boundless panic.
My lines end on a note of terror.
Yet it is good that this is so:
Those who are hard of heart—myself the
    first—
Are led to repentance, led to a holy life,
Less by the lure of blessings promised
Than by fearful warnings that inspire dread.
'He who has ears to hear, let him hear.'
You who have written this, hear, then, and take
    note:
Void of all these graces,
How have you dared to write such things?
How do you not shudder to expound them?

Have you not heard what Uzzah suffered
When he tried to stop God's ark from falling?
Do not think that I speak as one who teaches:
I speak as one whose words condemn himself,
Knowing the rewards awaiting those who
   strive,
Knowing my utter fruitlessness.

SAINT SYMEON METAPHRASTIS

Paraphrase of the Homilies of
Saint Makarios of Egypt

The Makarian Homilies were attributed in the past to St Makarios the Great of Egypt (*c.* 300–*c.* 390). A Coptic monk, priest and spiritual father in the desert of Sketis, he figures prominently in the *Lausiac History* of Palladios and in the *Sayings of the Desert Fathers,* and is commemorated in the Church's calendar on 19 January. But this ascription is open to doubt for many reasons: in particular, the early sources say nothing whatever about any writings by Makarios of Egypt, while the background presupposed by the Homilies is not

Egyptian but Syrian. All that can be said with any confidence is that the Homilies are the work of an unknown author, writing probably in Syria or Mesopotamia during the late fourth or the early fifth century.

While the Makarian Homilies do not underestimate the need for 'labour and sweat of the brow', what chiefly distinguishes them is their sense of communion with the Holy Spirit, and of the love and joy that He imparts. With their message of encouragement, their vigorous style and simple illustrations, it is not surprising that they should often be given as reading to novices at their first entry to the monastery.

Spiritual Perfection

I. We receive salvation by grace and as a divine gift of the Spirit. But to attain the full measure of virtue we need also to possess faith and love, and to struggle to exercise our free will with integrity. In this manner we inherit eternal life as a consequence of both grace and justice. We do not reach the final stage of spiritual maturity through divine power and grace alone, without ourselves making any effort; but neither on the other hand do we attain the final measure of freedom and purity as a result of our own diligence and strength alone, apart from any divine assistance. If the Lord does not build the house, it is said, and protect the city, in vain does the watchman keep awake, and in vain do the labourer and the builder work (cf. Ps. 127: 1–4).

2. What is the will of God that St Paul urges and invites each of us to attain (cf. 1 Thess. 4: 3)? It is total cleansing from sin, freedom from the shameful passions and the acquisition of the highest virtue. In other words, it is the purification and sanctification of the heart that comes about through fully experienced and conscious participation in the perfect and divine Spirit. 'Blessed are the pure in heart,' it is said, 'for they shall see God' (Matt. 5: 8); and again: 'Become perfect, as your heavenly Father is perfect' (Matt. 5: 48). And the psalmist says: 'Let my heart be unerring in Thy statutes, so that I am not ashamed' (Ps. 119: 80); and again: 'When I pay attention to all Thy commandments, then I will not be ashamed' (Ps. 119: 6). And to the person that asked, 'Who will ascend the Lord's hill, or who

will stand in His holy place?', the psalmist replied: 'He that has clean hands and a pure heart' (Ps. 24: 3–4), that is to say, he who has completely destroyed sin in act and thought.

3. The Holy Spirit, knowing that the unseen and secret passions are hard to get rid of—for they are as it were rooted in the soul—shows us through the psalmist how we can purify ourselves from them. 'Cleanse me from my secret faults', writes the psalmist (Ps. 19: 12), as though to say that through much prayer and faith, and by turning completely to God, we are able, with the help of the Spirit, to conquer them. But this is on condition that we too strive against them and keep strict watch over our heart (cf. Prov. 4: 23).

4. Moses indicates figuratively that the soul should not be divided in will between good and

evil, but should pursue the good alone; and that it must cultivate not the dual fruits of virtue and vice but those of virtue only. For he says: 'Do not yoke together on your threshing floor animals of a different species, such as ox and ass; but yoke together animals of the same species and so thresh your corn' (cf. Deut. 22: 10). This is to say, do not let virtue and vice work together on the threshing floor of your heart, but let virtue alone work there. Again he says: 'Do not weave flax into a woollen garment, or wool into a linen garment' (cf. Deut. 22: 11); and: 'Do not cultivate two kinds of fruit together on the same patch of your land' (cf. Deut. 22: 9). Similarly, you are not to mate an animal of one species with an animal of another species, but to mate like with like. All this is a concealed way of saying that you must

not cultivate virtue and vice together in yourself, but you must devote yourself singlemind-
edly to producing the fruits of virtue; and you
must not share your soul with two spirits—the
Spirit of God and the spirit of the world—but
you must give it solely to the Spirit of God and
must reap only the fruits of the Spirit. It is for
this reason that the psalmist writes: 'I have
prospered in all Thy commandments; I hate
every false way' (Ps. 119: 128).

5. The virgin soul that desires to be united
to God must keep itself pure not only from
overt sins like unchastity, murder, theft, gluttony, backbiting, falsity, avarice, greed and so
on; but to an even greater degree it must keep
itself pure from sins that are hidden, such as
desire, self-esteem, love of popularity, hypoc-
risy, love of power, wiliness, malice, hatred,

unbelief, envy, self-love, affectation and other things of this kind. According to Scripture, these concealed sins of the soul are just as pernicious as the overt sins. 'The Lord has scattered the bones of those who seek to please men', it says (Ps. 53: 5. LXX); and: 'The Lord will abhor the bloody and deceitful man' (Ps. 5: 6), thus making it clear that deceitfulness is just as abhorrent to God as murder. Again, it numbers among the 'workers of iniquity' those who 'speak peace to their neighbour but have evil in their hearts' (Ps. 28: 3), and elsewhere it speaks of those who commit lawless acts in their hearts (cf. Ps. 58: 2). It also says: 'Woe to you, when men speak well of you' (Luke 6: 26)—that is to say, when you want to hear people say good things about you and when you hang upon their glory and praise. It is true that those who do good cannot escape notice altogether. Indeed, the Lord Himself says: 'Let your light shine before men' (Matt. 5: 16), though here it is understood that we do good for the glory of God and not for our own glory or because we desire men's praise. If this is not the case, then we are lacking in faith, as the Lord makes clear when He says: 'How can you have faith when you receive honour from one another, and do not seek the honour that comes from the only God?' (John 5: 44). St Paul bids us to do everything, even to eat and to drink, for the glory of God; 'for,' he says, 'whether you eat or drink, or do anything else, do it for the glory of God' (1 Cor. 10: 31). And St John equates hatred with murder when he says: 'Whoever hates his brother is a murderer' (1 John 3: 15).

6. 'Love bears with all things, patiently ac-

cepts all things; love never fails' (1 Cor. 13: 7–8). This phrase 'never fails' makes it clear that, unless they have been granted total deliverance from the passions through the most complete and active love of the Spirit, even those who have received spiritual gifts are still liable to falter: they are still in danger, and must struggle in fear against the attacks launched on them by the spirits of evil. St Paul shows that not to be in danger of falling or liable to passion is such a lofty state that the tongues of angels, prophecy, all knowledge and gifts of healing are as nothing compared to it (cf. 1 Cor. 13: 1–8).

7. St Paul has here indicated the goal of perfection so that everyone, realizing his poverty in the face of such richness, may long for it intensely and may strive forward along the

spiritual path until he attains it. As has been said: 'Run, that you may reach your goal' (1 Cor. 9: 24).

8. To deny oneself (cf. Matt. 16: 24) is to be ready to give up everything for the brethren's sake and not to follow one's own will in anything, or to possess anything except one's own clothes. He who attains this state, and is thus freed from all things, joyfully does only what he is asked to do. He regards all the brethren, and especially the superiors and those appointed to bear the burdens of the monastery, as lords and masters for Christ's sake. In this way he obeys Christ who said: 'He among you who wants to be first and pre-eminent, let him be the last of all and the servant and slave of all' (cf. Mark 9: 35), not inviting any glory, honour or praise from the brethren for his service and

conduct. He serves the brethren with complete goodwill, with love and simplicity, not with outward show and with an eye to gaining popularity, but regarding himself as a debtor in everything.

9. The superiors of the community, who shoulder a great burden, must fight the crafty designs of evil with the weapon of humility, lest because of the authority they exercise over their subordinate brethren they grow proud and so act to their own detriment rather than to their profit. They should be like compassionate fathers, in the name of God giving themselves bodily and spiritually to the service of the community, keeping watch over the brethren and constantly looking after them as children of God. Outwardly they should not disown the rank of superior, as for instance in giving orders

or advice to the more experienced monks, or in punishing or rebuking someone when necessary, and in encouraging where it is appropriate; otherwise, on the grounds that they are being humble or gentle, they will introduce confusion into the monastery through not preserving the due order of superiors and subordinates. But inwardly, in their own minds, they should regard themselves as unworthy servants of all their brethren, and as teachers entrusted with the Lord's children; and with unreserved goodwill and fear of God they should do all they can to make each of the brethren apt for every good work, knowing that the reward they will receive from God for such labour will be great and inalienable.

10. There are times when servants whose task it is to instruct the young do not hesitate

in all charity to beat them for the sake of discipline or good behaviour, even if those they punish are the children of their own masters. Similarly, superiors should punish those of the brethren in need of discipline, yet not in anger or haughtiness, or for personal revenge, but with compassion and with a view to their reform and spiritual profit.

11. He who wants to be stamped with the virtues should pursue before everything else and at all times fear of God and holy love, the first and greatest of the commandments (cf. Matt. 22: 38). Let him continually beseech the Lord to send this love into his heart, and thus let him advance and grow, augmenting it by grace day by day through the ceaseless and unbroken remembrance of God. Through diligence and effort, concern and struggle he be-

comes capable of acquiring love for God, given form within him by the grace and bounty of Christ. Through such love the second commandment, love for one's neighbour (cf. Matt. 22: 39), can easily be attained. Let these two primary commandments take precedence over the others and let him pursue them more than the others. In this way the secondary commandments will follow naturally on the primary. But should he neglect this first and great commandment, the love for God that is formed with divine help from our inner disposition, our clear conscience and our life-giving remembrance of God, then in consequence of this neglect he cannot soundly and purely accomplish the second commandment, that requires simply the outward diligence of service. For the guile of evil, finding the intellect void of the remembrance of God, and of love and longing for Him, will make the divine commandments appear harsh and laborious, kindling in his soul grumbling, resentment and complaints about having to serve the brethren; or else it will deceive him with the presumption of self-righteousness, filling him with arrogance and making him think that he is of great importance and worthy of esteem, and that he has entirely fulfilled the commandments.

12. When a man thinks that he is keeping the commandments perfectly, it is obvious that he is mistaken and that he is breaking one of them, since he judges himself and does not submit to the true judge. But when, in St Paul's words (cf. Rom. 8: 16), the Spirit of God testifies along with our spirit, then indeed we are worthy of Christ and are children of God. This is not the

case, however, when we justify ourselves merely on the basis of what we ourselves think. It is not the man who commends himself that is to be trusted, but he whom Christ commends (cf. 2 Cor. 10: 18). When a man lacks the remembrance and fear of God, it is inevitable that he will long for glory and will seek for praise from those whom he serves. As has already been explained, such a person is called an unbeliever by Christ; for He says: 'How can you have faith when you receive honour from one another, and do not seek the honour that comes from the only God?' (John 5: 44).

13. As has been said, love for God can be attained through the intellect's great struggles and labours in holy meditation and in unremitting attention to all that is good. The devil, on the contrary, impedes our intellect, not letting

it devote itself to divine love through the remembrance of what is good, but enticing the senses with earthly desires. For the intellect that dwells undistractedly in the love and remembrance of God is the devil's death and, so to say, his noose. Hence it is only through the first commandment, love for God, that genuine love for one's brother can be established, and that true simplicity, gentleness, humility, integrity, goodness, prayer and the whole beautiful crown of the virtues can be perfected. Much struggle is needed, therefore, and much inward and unseen travail, much scrutiny of our thoughts and training of our soul's enfeebled organs of perception, before we can discriminate between good and evil, and strengthen and give fresh life to the afflicted powers of our soul through the diligent striving of our intellect towards God.

For by always cleaving to God in this way our intellect will become one spirit with the Lord, as St Paul puts it (cf. 1 Cor. 6: 17).

14. Those aspiring to the state of virtue must strive to fulfil the commandments by sustaining this inward struggle, travail and meditation unceasingly night and day, whether praying or serving, eating or drinking, or doing anything else. In this way, if any good comes about it will be to God's glory and not to their own. The fulfilment of the commandments presents no difficulty or trouble to us when it is facilitated by the love of God and when this love relieves it of all that is burdensome. As has been said, the whole effort of the enemy is directed towards distracting the intellect from the remembrance, fear and love of God, and to turning it by means of earthly forms and seductions away

from what is truly good towards what appears to be good.

15. The patriarch Abraham, when he was receiving Melchisedec, the priest of God, made him an offering from the firstfruits of the earth and so obtained his blessing (cf. Gen. 14: 19–20). Through this incident the Spirit indicates that the first and highest elements of our constitution—the intellect, the conscience, the loving power of the soul—must initially be offered to God as a holy sacrifice. The firstfruits and the highest of our true thoughts must be continually devoted to remembrance of Him, engrossed in His love and in unutterable and boundless longing for Him. In this way we can grow and move forward day by day, assisted by divine grace. Then the burden of fulfilling the commandments will appear light

to us, and we will carry them out faultlessly and irreproachably, helped by the Lord Himself on account of our faith in Him.

16. Where outward ascetic practice is concerned, which virtue is the most important? The answer to this is that the virtues are linked one to the other, and follow as it were a sacred sequence, one depending on the other. For instance, prayer is linked to love, love to joy, joy to gentleness, gentleness to humility, humility to service, service to hope, hope to faith, faith to obedience, and obedience to simplicity. Similarly, the vices are linked one to another: hatred to anger, anger to pride, pride to self-esteem, self-esteem to unbelief, unbelief to hardheartedness, hardheartedness to negligence, negligence to sluggishness, sluggishness

to apathy, apathy to listlessness, listlessness to lack of endurance, lack of endurance to self-indulgence, and so on with all the other vices.

17. The devil tries to soil and defile every good thing a man would do by intermingling with it his own seeds in the form of self-esteem, presumption, complaint, and other things of this kind, so that what we do is not done for God alone, or with a glad heart. Abel offered a sacrifice to God of the fat and firstlings of his flock, while Cain offered gifts of the fruits of the earth, but not of the firstfruits; and that is why God looked with favour on Abel's sacrifices, but paid no attention to Cain's gifts (cf. Gen. 4: 3–5). This shows us that it is possible to do something good in the wrong way—that is to say, to do it negligently, or scornfully, or

else not for God's sake but for some other purpose; and for this reason it is unacceptable to God.

Prayer

18. The crown of every good endeavour and the highest of achievements is diligence in prayer. Through it, God guiding us and lending a helping hand, we come to acquire the other virtues. It is in prayer that the saints experience communion in the hidden energy of God's holiness and inner union with it, and their intellect itself is brought through unutterable love into the presence of the Lord. 'Thou hast given gladness to my heart', wrote the psalmist (Ps. 4: 7); and the Lord Himself said that 'the kingdom of heaven is within you' (cf. Luke 17: 21). And what does the kingdom being within mean ex-

cept that the heavenly gladness of the Spirit is clearly stamped on the virtuous soul? For already in this life, through active communion in the Spirit, the virtuous soul receives a foretaste and a prelude of the delight, joy and spiritual gladness which the saints will enjoy in the eternal light of Christ's kingdom. This is something that St Paul also affirms: 'He consoles us in our afflictions, so that we can console others in every affliction through the consolation with which we ourselves have been consoled by God' (2 Cor. 1: 4). And passages in the Psalms likewise hint at this active gladness and consolation of the Spirit, such as: 'My heart and my flesh have rejoiced in the living God' (Ps. 84: 2. LXX); and: 'My soul will be filled with marrow and fatness' (Ps. 63: 5).

19. Just as the work of prayer is greater than

other work, so it demands greater effort and attention from the person ardently devoted to it, lest without him being aware the devil deprives him of it. The greater the good a person has in his care, the greater the attacks the devil launches on him; hence he must keep strict watch, so that fruits of love and humility, simplicity and goodness—and, along with them, fruits of discrimination—may grow daily from the constancy of his prayer. These will make evident his progress and increase in holiness, thus encouraging others to make similar efforts.

20. Not only does St Paul instruct us to pray without ceasing and to persist in prayer (cf. 1 Thess. 5: 17; Rom. 12: 12), but so also does the Lord when He says that God will vindicate those who cry out to Him day and night (cf. Luke 18: 7) and counsels us to 'watch and pray'

(Matt. 26: 41). We must therefore pray always and not lose heart (cf. Luke 18: 1). To put things more succinctly: he who persists in prayer has to struggle greatly and exert himself relentlessly if he is to overcome the many obstacles with which the devil tries to impede his diligence—obstacles such as sleep, listlessness, physical torpor, distraction of thought, confusion of intellect, debility, and so on, not to mention afflictions, and also the attacks of the evil spirits that violently fight against us, opposing us and trying to prevent the soul from approaching God when it truly and ceaselessly seeks Him.

21. He who cultivates prayer has to fight with all diligence and watchfulness, all endurance, all struggle of soul and toil of body, so that he does not become sluggish and surrender

himself to distraction of thought, to excessive sleep, to listlessness, debility and confusion, or defile himself with turbulent and indecent suggestions, yielding his mind to things of this kind, satisfied merely with standing or kneeling for a long time, while his intellect wanders far away. For unless a person has been trained in strict vigilance, so that when attacked by a flood of useless thoughts he tests and sifts them all, yearning always for the Lord, he is readily seduced in many unseen ways by the devil. Moreover, those not yet capable of persisting in prayer can easily grow arrogant, thus allowing the machinations of evil to destroy the good work in which they are engaged and making a present of it to the devil.

22. Unless humility and love, simplicity and goodness regulate our prayer, this prayer—or,

rather, this pretence of prayer—cannot profit us at all. And this applies not only to prayer, but to every labour and hardship undertaken for the sake of virtue, whether this be virginity, fasting, vigil, psalmody, service or any other work. If we do not see in ourselves the fruits of love, peace, joy, simplicity, humility, gentleness, guilelessness, faith, forbearance and kindliness, then we endure our hardship to no purpose. We accept the hardships in order to reap the fruits. If the fruits of love are not in us, our labour is useless. In such a case we differ in nothing from the five foolish virgins: because their hearts were not filled here and now, in this present life, with spiritual oil—that is to say, with the energy of the Spirit active in the virtues of which we have spoken—they were called fools and were abjectly excluded from the royal bridechamber, not enjoying any reward for their efforts to preserve their virginity (cf. Matt. 25: 1–13). When we cultivate a vineyard, the whole of our attention and labour is given in the expectation of the vintage; if there is no vintage, all our work is to no purpose. Similarly, if through the activity of the Spirit we do not perceive within ourselves the fruits of love, peace, joy and the other qualities mentioned by St Paul (cf. Gal. 5: 22), and cannot affirm this with all assurance and spiritual awareness, then our labour for the sake of virginity, prayer, psalmody, fasting and vigil is useless. For, as we said, our labours and hardships of soul and body should be undertaken in expectation of the spiritual harvest; and where the virtues are concerned, the harvest consists of spiritual enjoyment and incorruptible pleasure secretly made active by the Spirit in faithful and humble hearts. Thus the labours and hardships must be regarded as labours and hardships and the fruits as fruits. Should someone through lack of spiritual knowledge think that his work and hardship are fruits of the Spirit, he should realize that he is deluding himself, and in this way depriving himself of the truly great fruits of the Spirit.

23. The person who has surrendered himself entirely to sin indulges with enjoyment and pleasure in unnatural and shameful passions—licentiousness, unchastity, greed, hatred, guile and other forms of vice—as though they were natural. The genuine and perfected Christian, on the other hand, with great enjoyment and spiritual pleasure participates effortlessly and without impediment in all the virtues and all

the supranatural fruits of the Spirit—love, peace, patient endurance, faith, humility and the entire truly golden galaxy of virtue—as though they were natural. He does not fight any longer against the passions of evil, for he has been totally set free of them by the Lord; while from the blessed Spirit he has received Christ's perfect peace and joy in his heart. Of such a man it may be said that he cleaves to the Lord and has become one spirit with Him (cf. 1 Cor. 6: 17).

24. Those who because of their spiritual immaturity cannot yet commit themselves entirely to the work of prayer should undertake to serve the brethren with reverence, faith and devout fear. They should do this because they regard such service as a divine commandment and a spiritual task; they should not expect

reward, honour or thanks from men, and they should shun all complaint, haughtiness, negligence or sluggishness. In this way they will not soil and corrupt this blessed work, but through their reverence, fear and joy will make it acceptable to God.

25. The Lord descended to the human level with such love, goodness and divine compassion for us, that He took it upon Himself not to overlook the reward of any good work, but to lead us step by step from the small to the great virtues, so that not even a cup of cold water should go unrequited. For He said: 'If anyone gives even a cup of cold water to someone simply in the name of a disciple, I tell you truly that he will not go unrewarded' (cf. Matt. 10: 42); and elsewhere: 'Whatever you did to one of these, you did to Me' (cf. Matt. 25: 40).

Only the action must be done in the name of God, not for the sake of receiving honour from men: the Lord said, 'simply in the name of a disciple', that is to say, in the fear and love of Christ. Those who do good with ostentation are rebuked categorically by the Lord: 'I tell you truly, they have received their reward' (Matt. 6: 2).

26. Simplicity before others, guilelessness, mutual love, joy and humility of every kind, must be laid down as the foundation of the community. Otherwise, disparaging others or grumbling about them, we make our labour profitless. He who persists ceaselessly in prayer must not disparage the man incapable of doing this, nor must the man who devotes himself to serving the needs of the community complain about those who are dedicated to prayer. For if

both the prayers and the service are offered in a spirit of simplicity and love for others, the superabundance of those dedicated to prayer will make up for the insufficiency of those who serve, and *vice versa*. In this way the equality that St Paul commends is maintained (cf. 2 Cor. 8: 14): he who has much does not have to excess and he who has little has no lack (cf. Exod. 16: 18).

27. God's will is done on earth as in heaven when, in the way indicated, we do not disparage one another, and when not only are we without jealousy but we are united one to another in simplicity and in mutual love, peace and joy, and regard our brother's progress as our own and his failure as our loss.

28. He who is sluggish in prayer, and slothful and negligent in serving his brethren and in

performing other holy tasks, is explicitly called an idler by the apostle, and condemned as unworthy even of his bread. For St Paul writes that the idler is not to have any food (cf. 2 Thess. 3: 10); and elsewhere it is said that God hates idlers, that the idle man cannot be trusted, and that idleness has taught great evil (cf. Ecclus. 33: 27). Thus each of us should bear the fruit of some action performed in God's name, even if he has employed himself diligently in but one good work. Otherwise he will be totally barren, and without any share in eternal blessings.

29. When people say that it is impossible to attain perfection, to be once and for all free from the passions, or to participate fully in the Holy Spirit, we should cite Holy Scripture against them, showing them that they are igno-

rant and speak falsely and dangerously. For the Lord said: 'Become perfect, as your heavenly Father is perfect' (Matt. 5: 48), perfection denoting total purity; and: 'I desire these men to be with Me wherever I am, so that they may see My glory' (John 17: 24). He also said: 'Heaven and earth will pass away, but My words will not pass away' (Matt. 24: 35). And St Paul is saying the same as Christ when he writes: '. . . so that we may present every man perfect in Christ' (Col. 1: 28); and: '. . . until we all attain to the unity of the faith and of the knowledge of the Son of God, to a perfect man, to the measure of the stature of the fulness of Christ' (Eph. 4: 13). Thus by aspiring to perfection two of the best things come about, provided we struggle diligently and unceasingly: we seek to attain this perfect measure and growth; and we are

not conquered by vanity, but look upon ourselves as petty and mean because we have not
yet reached our goal.

30. Those who deny the possibility of perfection inflict the greatest damage on the soul
in three ways. First, they manifestly disbelieve
the inspired Scriptures. Then, because they do
not make the greatest and fullest goal of Chris-
tianity their own, and so do not aspire to attain
it, they can have no longing and diligence, no
hunger and thirst for righteousness (cf. Matt. 5:
6); on the contrary, content with outward show
and behaviour and with minor accomplish-
ments of this kind, they abandon that blessed
expectation together with the pursuit of perfection and of the total purification of the passions. Third, thinking they have reached the
goal when they have acquired a few virtues, and

not pressing on to the true goal, not only are they incapable of having any humility, poverty and contrition of heart but, justifying themselves on the grounds that they have already arrived, they make no efforts to progress and grow day by day.

31. People who think it is impossible to attain through the Spirit the 'new creation' of the pure heart (cf. 2 Cor. 5: 17) are rightly and explicitly likened by the apostle to those who, because of their unbelief, were found unworthy of entering the promised land and whose bodies on that account 'were left lying in the desert' (Heb. 3: 17). What is here outwardly described as the promised land signifies inwardly that deliverance from the passions which the apostle regards as the goal of every commandment. This is the true promised land, and for its sake

these figurative teachings have been handed down. In order to protect his disciples from yielding to unbelief the apostle says to them: 'Make sure, my brethren, that no one among you has an evil heart of unbelief, turning away from the living God' (Heb. 3: 12). By 'turning away' he means not the denial of God but disbelief in His promises. Interpreting the events of Jewish history allegorically and indicating their true meaning, he says: 'For some, when they heard, were rebellious, though not all of those who were brought out of Egypt by Moses. And with whom was God angry for forty years? Was it not with those who had sinned, whose bodies were left lying in the desert? And to whom did He vow that they would not enter into His rest unless it was to those who refused to believe? We see, then, that it was because of their unbelief that they could not enter' (Heb. 3: 16–19). And he continues: 'Let us be fearful, then: although the promise of entering into His rest still holds good, some of you may be excluded from it. For we have heard the divine message, as they did; but the message that they heard did not profit them, since it was not accompanied by faith on their part. We, however, who have faith do enter into God's rest' (Heb. 4: 1–3). Shortly after this he draws the same conclusion: 'Let us strive therefore to enter into that rest, so that no one may fall through copying this example of unbelief' (Heb. 4: 11). For Christians what true rest is there other than deliverance from the sinful passions and the fullest active indwelling of the Holy Spirit in the purified heart? And the apostle again impels his readers towards this by referring to faith: 'Let us then draw near with a true heart and in the full assurance of faith, our hearts cleansed of an evil conscience' (Heb. 10: 22). And again: 'How much more will the blood of Jesus purge our conscience of dead works, so that we may serve the living and true God' (cf. Heb. 9: 14). Because of the measureless blessings promised by God to men in these words, we should dedicate ourselves as grateful servants and regard what is promised as true and certain. In this way, even if through sluggishness or debility of resolution we do not give ourselves once for all to our Maker, or if we do not strive to achieve the greatest and most perfect measure of virtue, none the less through an upright and undistorted will and a sound faith we may attain some degree of mercy.

32. Prayer rightly combined with understanding is superior to every virtue and commandment. The Lord Himself testifies to this. For in the house of Martha and Mary He contrasted Martha, who was engaged in looking after Him, with Mary, who sat at His feet joyfully drinking the ambrosia of His divine words. When Martha complained and appealed to Christ, He made clear to her what takes precedence, saying: 'Martha, Martha, you are anxious and troubled about many things; one thing alone is needful: Mary has chosen what is best, and it cannot be taken away from her' (Luke 10: 41–42). He said this not in order to disparage acts of service, but so as to distinguish clearly what is higher from what is lower. For how could He not give His sanction to service when He Himself performed such ser-

vice in washing His disciples' feet, and was so far from discountenancing it that He bade His disciples to behave in the same way towards each other (cf. John 13: 4–16)? Moreover, the apostles themselves, when they were oppressed by serving at table, also singled out prayer and understanding as the higher form of work. 'It is not right', they said, 'for us to abandon the word of God in order to serve at table. Let us appoint chosen men, full of the Holy Spirit, for this service; we will devote ourselves to the ministry of the Logos and to prayer' (cf. Acts 6: 2–4). In this way they put first things before secondary things, although they recognized that both spring from the same blessed root.

Library of Congress Cataloging-in-Publication Data
Philokalia. English. Selections.
    Prayer of the heart: writings from the Philokalia: from
the complete text/compiled by Saint Nikodimos of·the Holy
Mountain and Saint Makarios of Corinth: translated from the
Greek and edited by G.E.H. Palmer, Philip Sherrard, and
Kallistos Ware. —1st ed.
        p.   cm. —(Shambhala centaur editions)
    ISBN 0-87773-890-4 (pbk.: alk. paper)
    1. Spiritual life—Orthodox Eastern Church.   2. Asceticism—
Orthodox Eastern Church.   3. Orthodox Eastern Church—
Doctrines.   I. Nicodemus, the Hagiorite, Saint, 1748–1809.
II. Markaios, Saint, Metropolitan of Corinth, 1731–1805.
III. Palmer, G. E. H. (Gerald Eustace Howell), 1904–   .
VI. Title.   Philip.   V. Ware, Kallistos, 1934–   .
VI. Title.   VII. Series
BX382.P42513   1993
248.4'819—dc20   92-56453
CIP

SHAMBHALA CENTAUR EDITIONS are named for a classical modern typeface designed by the eminent American typographer Bruce Rogers. Modeled on a fifteenth-century Roman type, Centaur was originally an exclusive titling font for the Metropolitan Museum of Art, New York. The first book in which it appeared was Maurice de Guérin's *The Centaur*, printed in 1915. Until recently, Centaur type was available only for handset books printed on letterpress. Its elegance and clarity make it the typeface of choice for Shambhala Centaur Editions, which include outstanding classics of the world's literary and spiritual traditions.